O'Neil Ford Duograph 4: México

Ajijic House, 2009-2011
Tatiana Bilbao

CB29 Apartments, 2005-2007
Dellekamp Arquitectos

The O'Neil Ford Duograph Series, Volume 4
– México
Ajijic House and CB29 Apartments

THE UNIVERSITY OF TEXAS AT AUSTIN
Center for American Architecture and Design
O'Neil Ford Chair in Architecture

Editor
Wilfried Wang

Essays
Patrick Charpenel
Tatiana Bilbao
Fernanda Canales
Yoaci Pardo
Derek Dellekamp
Wilfried Wang

Translation
Michael W. Parker Stainback

Series Editors
Kevin Alter
Michael Benedikt
Barbara Hoidn
Wilfried Wang

Production Editors
Susan McNally
Leora Visotzky

Typographic Design
Tyler Collins

Cover Photographs
Iwan Baan

Printed and bound in Canada.

Sole Distributor in Europe:
Ernst Wasmuth Verlag GmbH & Co.
D-72072 Tübingen, Germany
www.wasmuth-verlag.de
info@wasmuth-verlag.de

ISBN 978-3-8030-0741-4

Sole Distributor in the United States of America and Canada
D.A.P. / Distributed Art Publishers
155 Sixth Avenue, 2nd Floor
New York, New York 10013, U.S.A.
Tel. (212) 627-1999, Fax. (212) 67-9484

Contents

House on a slope

Beyond Dogma

Wilfried Wang

Since the inception of the O'Neil Ford Duograph series, it has been the editors' intention to dedicate one volume a year to contemporary architects whose work merits international attention. Thus far, there have been three volumes focusing on South American countries: Chile, Brazil and Argentina. With this present volume, we are for the first time publishing two buildings from a North America country, namely México.

Following the Saul-Steinbergian worldview, an ironic parochial perspective that summarizes the minds of many inhabitants of the northern hemisphere, México is seen as part of South America; in cultural terms it certainly is part of so-called Latin America. From the perspective of the rich North, México is seen as the beginning of South America. As false as this segregation is in geographical terms, so it is indicative of the hegemonic attitude of the North. Despite its enormous sovereing debt, the USA is still considered a wealthy nation on the strength of its productivity; México on the other hand is still considered as poor, though it has the world's 13th largest nominal gross domestic product according to the World Bank (2010). The actual figures of the two countries' gross domestic product seem to say it all: USA at U$ 14,528,400 million, México at U$ 1,039,662 million. But these economic indicators and the often-idealized cultural differences between North and South America, between the USA and Latin America, are not so clean cut as many Anglo-Saxon Americans would like to believe. The continuities between South, Central and North America are far stronger, particularly in the broader cultural realm, than the differences in headline gross domestic product of each nation.

This cultural continuity is clearly visible in the double continent's built culture. The leitmotif of the central business districts with their object-like high rises surrounded by a network of motorways and suburbs unifies the Americas. Delving deeper into the quotidian reality of this settlement culture, many of the decrepit aspects of the constructed environment are seamlessly present from Chile and Argentina in the South to the USA and Canada in the North. Degraded infrastructure can be witnessed across the Americas: exposed reinforcement bars lurking beneath still heavily used concrete bridges; obsolescent suburbia gradually dilapidating as much as a result of the cheap materials and construction details used as for the lack of care and maintenance for these lightweight huts; overhead jumbled cables for electricity and telecommunications everywhere, so frequently the object of nature's destructive powers, uncoupling thousands from services that are second nature to otherwise comfort-spoiled "advanced" societies. Conversely and equally everywhere can be found downtowns filled with the same intensively serviced, inappropriately glazed high rises. Along the strip malls one sees disproportionately large layers of ever-garish adverts standing in front, between and on top of buildings, establishing an entirely different order of spatial perception that is closer to the speed and space of the automobile than to the urban flaneur. Beneath all of these omnipresent decrepit facts the contemporary omnibus-archaeologist will uncover remnants of pre-automobile cultures that are far more telling of the indigenous societies than the superficial differences in the language of advertising.

When these settlements and their infrastructures are experienced in combination with their "application systems", be they modes of transport (mostly private bus operators and private automobiles), or utilities and communication networks, their creaking and declining nature becomes all the more apparent. None of these systems are designed to last for more than a few decades, though just long enough for private enterprises to have installed one generation of technology and to reap their rewards only to relinquish the responsibility for the ageing systems to the next generation of entrepreneurs or, in the last resort, the public realm. From motorway bridges to communication networks, from schools to health facilities, and from public spaces to cultural institutions, the presence of the sovereign public has been in retreat in the Americas for the last four decades, no reverse in the trend being in sight.

For American architects the consequences of this state of affairs have been twofold: the effective circumscription of their commissions to private residences, speculative housing and commercial development and the growth in the public's perception of the architectural profession as servants to the wealthy. Business parks, shopping malls with ever the same set of retailers, conspicuously large and expensive single-family houses in homogeneous suburbs, and smaller villas in gated communities have been the architects' staple diet and stable commissions over the last half a century. The advance of the private domain in the appropriation of the environment shows no signs of diminution. It cannot then surprise anyone, that, at the macro-level, that is to say, between nation states, similar segregating techniques are being employed.

Given the nominally steep gradient between the economies of México and the USA, the border between them has become more than a physical last line of defense for a gated community at a national level. It is a symbol of the idealized difference between the USA and how this nation views itself. All the same, amongst the Latin American countries, México is only second to Brazil in terms of economic dynamism.

Despite the barbed wire constructed on the USA side of the border, this idealized cultural barrier will be as effective as the once unguarded shores of the former Native American East Coast, now called Massachusetts, against the arrival of English pilgrims in the early 17th century, legal or otherwise. Sealing the USA-México border is a futile project as continuities beyond the built environment have long ago established themselves across this border. The Hispanics are projected to constitute a quarter of the total population of the USA by the year 2050. More important has been the existing regional presence of Hispanics in US American states close to México (California, Arizona, New Mexico and Texas; Colorado, Nevada, New York and Florida), where in four decades time the Hispanic segment of the population will be closer to a half of the total local population (even with the barbed wire fence).

Thus the reality on the ground and its projected development (according to the Census Bureau of the USA) is unfolding regardless of the physical and cultural segregation between the regions. More generally, what stretches across the Americas in terms of the built environment is and will be more uniform in terms of its settlement typologies even in its multi-ethnic and multi-cultural variety than many of those who would prefer to uphold differences believe. So, while Hispanics in the USA continue to suffer social discrimination, and while cheap laborers and many immigrants to the USA are Spanish speakers, the perception of Hispanics and their culture is destined to change, albeit gradually.

With the northern hemisphere's self-satisfaction with its culture and the resultant collateral ignorance of cultural matters in Asia, Africa and South America, and with the hegemonic role played by Anglo-Saxon culture as a product of the current global acceptance of English as the lingua franca, it becomes all the more important to acknowledge contributions to the international architectural discourse when and where it occurs. This Duograph on México in particular, as the Duograph series in general, is intended to contribute to this changing cultural perception of Latin America by the northern hemisphere.

Beyond Dogma

The criteria for selection of noteworthy architecture are not determined by the quasi-late colonial, quasi-touristic mindset that has as its ideal the unspoilt homogeneity of pre-industrialized vernacular, but the same critical basis on which any other building from anywhere else should be judged. This critique seeks to understand the intentions motivating the realization of a building, its physical and cultural context, as well as its architectural-compositional, physiological and cultural integrity, before it reaches a conclusion regarding the contribution such an evaluated building makes to the global, regional and local discourses. The selection of Tatiana Bilbao's Ajijic House and Derek Dellekamp's CB29 Apartments in México City will be presented in these terms.

Wider discussions, especially the more introverted ones focusing on architecture's language and style as seemingly determined by construction systems and materials, processes of industrialization, economic rationalism, functional necessities, social needs, in short, on modernism as distinct from any language developed from tradition (either Pre-Hispanic or Spanish Colonial), have preoccupied Mexican architects as much as colleagues in other countries. The resulting environment, as mentioned above, is a tribute to the power of economic rationalism on the one hand and to scenographic escapism on the other hand as seen in continued repetition of variations on the Pre-Hispanic or Spanish Colonial styles. In broad terms, modernization can be argued to include the eradication of indigenous value systems and their replacement by those of the socio-political dominators. In México, as in all regions of the American continent, religious belief, languages, patterns of subsistence, modes of food preparation, building typologies and settlement patterns were affected to varying degrees; some of these cultural phenomena survive more or less intact, some only in vestigial form, others exist as decontextualized fragments in museums.

Three centuries of colonial rule and two centuries of gradual attempts at gaining a sense of socio-political autonomy, marred by humiliating losses of territory to its northern neighbor, México has faced similar fundamental questions regarding its own self-understanding as any other country around the world. The now firmly established economic rationalism coupled with the escapist view of the superficial stylistic repetition of once stable times is a socio-cultural pattern common not only to México, but to the globe. The role of urban and architectural modernism in the process of the diminution, erasure and replacement of indigenous value systems is rarely discussed in its problematic, collaborative dimension. By the beginning of the 21st century, the origins of dogmatic urban and architectural modernism have as much a historic perspective as other historical models. Contemporary architects in México, with indigenous roots or not, and certainly more so than architects in Europe, invariably confront themselves with the question as to the legitimacy of imposed and imported systems, which of the vestiges of previous indigenous value systems have retained their relevance and legitimacy, and how to make sense of the partial answers, how to find a synthetic position that in itself possesses a broad comprehensibility.

A noble and grand attempt at reconciling the sheer force of modernization on the one hand and the longing for broad comprehensibility on the other may be seen at the Universidad

Augusto Pérez Palacios, Rául Salinas, Jorge Bravo, Olympic Stadium, UNAM, México City, 1952

Nacional Autónoma de México (México City, 1949-1952, numerous architects (150) including Teodoro González de León, Armando Franco Rovira, Enrique Molinar, Mario Pani, Enrique del Moral, Juan O'Gorman, Domingo García Ramos, and murals amongst others by Diego Rivera and David Alfaro Siquieros; since 2007, the main campus is listed as part of the UNESCO World Heritage). Monumental in scale, integrating the spatial concepts of Aztec temple precincts with the typology of a campus university, the project proved Mexico's ability to plan and realize large institutions, securing it in 1963 the 1968 Olympic Games (until Rio de Janeiro's successful bid for the 2016 Games, México was the only Latin American host country). The inclusion of images in architecture at this scale with explicit reference to local history is quite without parallel in the immediate post Second World War years.

Diego Rivera's dream of reconciling the emancipated people with its ancient tradition by means of the various murals for UNAM as well as his painterly oeuvre represents the dilemma of the artists living in two worlds: the quotidian here and now and the wider context of the contortions of history and the challenges posed by the world outside. The here and now calls for immediacy, the recourse to commonly used media and broadly understood languages. The wider context increases the degree of complexity, densifies the message. Artists, like architects, intend their works to have a general applicability, a universal value. At the same time, especially artists are driven by the western concept of originality, requiring each work to be unique. The dilemma posed by the potentially conflicting goals of immediacy on the one hand and originality on the other can be a cause for frustration and desperation. The engendered anxiety may appear unresolvable. However, especially in the realm of architecture, the *répetition differente* permits gradual evolution, the absorption of tried and tested solutions with selective corrections and developments.

Diego Rivera's mural project for the 1968 Olympic Stadium at UNAM was left incomplete due to his untimely death. However, as Alberto Kalach observes , this fragment may have allowed the stadium to retain its topographic immediacy, appearing itself as if it were part of the Xitle volcano, on which a segment of

Mario Pani, Unidad Habitacional Nonoalcol-Tlatelolco, México City 1960-65

the university is sited. Kalach further observes that the stadium's architects, Augusto Pérez Palacios, Raúl Salinas and Jorge Bravo, were forced to amend their original structural concept of a reinforced concrete building for cost and technological reasons to one that would make use of the on-site material of Tepetate (Spanish for the Mexican term Nahuatl tepetlatl), brittle volcanic rock, to form a series of epic terraces (the university stadium was completed in 1952). Thus, a rare conjunction of a new function and powerful topography was made using the material of the place. Kalach writes: "The absolute correspondence between space, structure and function surpasses any notion of style, while only a few accents in the stadium leave a trace of the epoch. ... This landscape architecture recalls the silent and archaic permanence of the pre-Hispanic era, yet it also has the rational spirit of Modern architecture."

Mario Pani's design for the Unidad Habitacional Nonoalcol-Tlatelolco (México City, 1960-65) was another rare opportunity at requiting a modern mass-housing scheme including the neighborhood's communal needs with pre-existing buildings, in this case the archaeological remains of the Aztec ceremonial center of a market city and the colonial church of Santiago Tlatelolco, built on an early 16th century battle site. Pani's modernist neo-plastic composition was ideally suited to connect the new layer with the old: retaining walls, both old and new, slabs of buildings whether containing housing or the former church engaged in spatial conversations (many of the high-rise elements had to be demolished as the 1985 earthquake made most of them unfit for use), Aztec terraces with the new architectural landscape.

The precedent for the approach underlying these three cases could be argued to have been Luís Barragán's Jardines del Pedregal in México City (begun in the mid-1940s, that includes a demonstration house and a demonstration garden by Max Cetto, as well as the sculpture Animal del Pedegral by Mathias Goeritz), located south of the UNAM campus. With a few judicious additions that clearly spoke of their artificial character, be they buildings or architectural landscape elements, the extent of the pre-existing lava rocks were complemented and turned into the project's protagonist.

These selected built discourses of a small group of intense architects needs to be seen, as in every country, whether developed, developing or not, against the vast background of non-architect designed and built edifices. The observer from the northern hemisphere may not suspect this, but México City with its expanse of self-built house construction is more homogeneous than, say, the vast tracts of unthinkingly composed and poorly built structures along France's Côte d'Azur or the suburban belt around London. México's contemporary dominant vernacular is a synthesis of courtyard types and clear street grids. In the country's capital, around the turn of the 21st century, the once distant framing hills have been reached and encroached by such building types. At the edge of the city, exploring the topographic changes, taller speculative residential units take advantage of the views across the flat expanse. Here, a second order dense urbanism has developed, one that matches the imposition of inner city motorways, the latter having been dropped into its context as sensitively as an axe is struck against a tree, as seen with the Viaducto Elevado Bicentenario, the raised motorway completed in 2010.

If México's northern neighbors have effectively embraced multi-culturalism, the lingering ideal of a national architecture with distinct Mexican character somehow synthesized from past periods and contemporary technology remains strong amongst some architectural observers. Most of the architecture in México that is being constructed in the first decade of the 21st century, in distinction to the urban vernacular as mentioned above, could not be further from this sentimental ideal. In fact, the most noteworthy buildings being realized in México is closer to global practice. Literal rootedness to the ground, the use of local materials as demonstrated at Jardines del Pedregal, the use of earth in compacted form, can be seen now and again in contemporary practice, though it is many conceptual steps removed from the Aztec concept of linking the earth to the sky by means of their terraced structures. Mauricio Rocha's Oaxaca School of Plastic Arts (2008) expresses this developed position well: its general layout carries echoes of Pre-Hispanic earthworks, the use of reinforced concrete permits the extensive use of the lower floors. The artist Gabriel Orozco's Universe Beach House (inspired by the Jantar Mantar astronomical observatory in Delhi, 1724), jointly designed with Tatiana Bilbao (2007), brings together concepts of square plan terrace structures, Pre-Hispanic cosmology (the hemispherical pool at the center of the roof terrace), the centredness of such follies as the Villa Rotonda (1566-76) and platforms such as that of the Villa Malaparte (1938-42). At the opposite end of the spectrum of structural concepts is Alberto Kalach's Vasconcelos Library in México City (2004-07) with its suspended stacks that are hung from a linearly extruded pyramidal frame. Certainly these three cases do not exhaust the range of 21st century architecture in México; they are nevertheless paradigms of their respective types.

Today, the architectural discourse in México itself is striated in terms of building types, sophisticated in terms of material and formal articulation and exhausted by the constant international reference to one or two noteworthy architects. It is true that like many countries around the world, regardless of their developmental status, the constructional and compositional systems moved seamlessly from the Beaux-Arts mode to Modernism (Beaux-Arts minus the ornament equalled academic modernism). In México, the pedagogic impact of Juan O'Gorman and Hannes Meyer (the shunned Bauhaus Director) at the Instituto Politécnico Nacional during the 1930s had a lasting impact on the thinking and making of buildings in México. Dogmatic Modernism was effectively taught until the end of the 20th century. This impact helps in part to explain a certain predilection by some corporate practices for bold, geometrically based configurations.

Like Finland (with Alvar Aalto) and Portugal (with Álvaro Siza), entire stylistic schools have established themselves to participate in the marketability of their modern architectural heroes. If Aalto and Siza were each successful in synthesizing social conditions, construction techniques, and traditions in art with cultural aspirations of an entire nation, then the external reading of Mexican architecture would idealistically ascribe similar qualities to Luís Barragán's work. While this latter work is still a necessary touchstone for the younger generation of architects in México, it no longer is an all-determining reference. Such a departure from the architectural heroes of the 20th century is a consequence of the reality on the ground attracting more attention than the unstructured images that are available from all over the world. Of course there are the many commissions for free standing houses, on which the models of the early moderns may still have a formative impact. However, there is also a wealth of building commissions that challenge the conceptual inventiveness of recent generations of Mexican architects. Complex urban sites or mixed-use developments present tasks for which there are few ready-made answers from Modernist case studies.

A further aspect in the revaluation of the "reality on the ground" is the research into important traditions and bodies of work by other colleagues, both historic and contemporary. Thus for example, upon reviewing the larger body of the respective oeuvre, neither Juan O'Gorman nor Mario Pani's positions can be reduced to that of dogmatic modernists, positions that would otherwise have been deduced from the selective view of their better-known buildings. O'Gorman's late work became engaged with and intensive vernacular (his own house for Jardines del Pedregal, 1951); Pani explored spatial plasticity beyond orthogonal geometry. Enrique del Moral, like a small number of architects across the globe, were reacting to the alienating aesthetic of industrialized production methods (see his own house of

Ajijic House

1948 in Tacubaya, México City, a synthesis of vernacular materials and modernist spatial composition like Knut Knutsen's summer house in Portør (1949), Norway, Fernando Tavora's Tennis Pavilion in Matosinhos (1957) or his Summer House at Ofir (1957-58), Portugal). Thus, from the orthodox, dogmatic Modernism taught at schools of architecture in México throughout the last eight decades, a diverse and

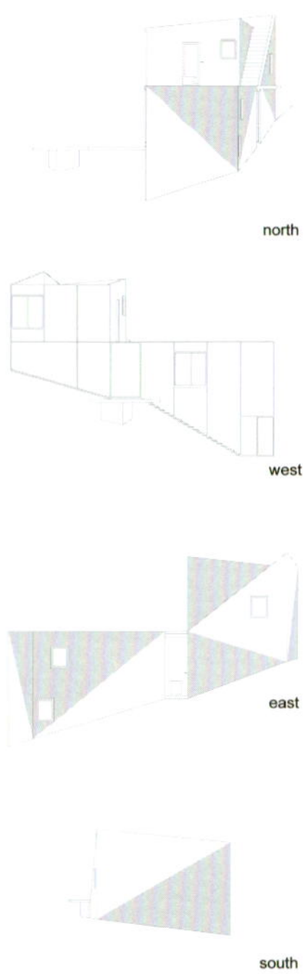

House on a slope

adaptable real Modernism has emerged as a result of interested architects confronting the breadth of their colleague's building activities. The dogmatic Modernism, so often upheld by the self-professed standard-bearers from academe, has long been superseded. Tatiana Bilbao and Derek Dellekamp's buildings, especially the two presented in this Duograph, are telling cases in undogmatic modern architecture.

New realities on the ground

Given the complex programs and sites, and given the diverse and adaptable reality, these issues are not meant to pave the way for a value-free or unprincipled pragmatism. Just as for the artist there is superficially the irresolvable dilemma of the uniqueness of the work versus the artist's concern for universal comprehensibility, so for architects there is a similar superficial dilemma of the universality of a design, quasi a generally valid model for the world, versus its originality, and hence specificity to its site and program.

It is then Tatiana Bilbao's approach to the design of the Ajijic House that is the generally transferable part of the design. The site is unique and privileged: the house marks the edge of a lake, the edge of a rectangular plot, the edge between the approach and the view. The materials, compacted earth, are not ubiquitously applicable. However, what is transferable is the notion of the internal reference, or the self-referential mode, in which one half of the house is in conversation with the other, just like Tatiana Bilbao's Ordos House of 2008, that is quasi split across a diagonal, as if separated, pulled apart leaving two sets of stepped walls. The architecture of the Ajijic House thus becomes a didactic frame that makes the users aware of the other: public and collective versus private and individual, view towards the hills versus views towards the lake. In a way, one could argue, this formal reference also exists in the relationship between the hemispherical pool of the Orozco Universe Beach House vis-à-vis the idealized domed sky.

In a world that appears to lack references in cultural terms, in which our actions are no longer restricted or guided by aesthetic or ethical codes, the recourse to universally comprehensible primary references, even if auto-referential, seems the better course in revalidating architecture than the path to ever greater complexity, intellectual sophistication or even sophistry. That there is a magical simplicity to the auto-referential can be seen in Erwin Heerich's sculptures and exhibition buildings (1978-2004) for the Museum Island at Hombroich, Germany. Besides their direct materiality, their formal articulation is such that the compositional logic of each form and building becomes self-evident to the observer. As with Bilbao's houses, the concept for each configuration "unfolds" by simply reading it.

Derek Dellekamp, Living room, House on a slope, México City

Derek Dellekamp shared this approach, an interest that can be seen well in Dellekamp's first "House on a Slope" on the outskirts of México City, Desierto de Los Leones (2003). Here, the configuration is treated as if there were a rotational symmetry about the second level, with the first and third levels acting as quiet counterpoints. The triangulated pattern on the eastern walls with the two different grey colors have the effect of reducing the size of the house in the manner of naval dazzle paints. In another

way, the overall image is distantly reminiscent of Jacques Tati's modern house in the movie Mon Oncle, with the windows of the "House on the Slope" on either side of the main entrance (as the nose) forming anthropomorphic eyes.
As a first project in design economy, the "House on a Slope" consists of all the elements of subsequent apartment buildings designed by Derek Dellekamp: U-shaped masonry enclosure with curtain glazing (even if the "House on a Slope" has to make do with the cheapest, and not necessarily most elegant profiles), spatial explorations such as diagonal views, double height volumes, tight sanitary planning. Dellekamp knows how to master the logic of construction and still distill figurative moments from this. For both Dellekamp and Bilbao, architecture is not merely nerdy construction, although it has its constituting raison d'être in this discipline, but the wringing and massing of spatial and configurative expression, be it within the building itself as a auto-referential statement or in relation to larger contexts.

Derek Dellekamp's series of apartments for México City are each careful readings of their respective sites. While a more commercially oriented office might be prone to apply "tried and tested" solutions that the "market wants", effectively using standard typologies and construction details, Dellekamp and his clients take significant risks in experimenting with apartment typologies. His first apartment building on Calle Alfonso Reyes 58 (2000-03) provides for a different unit on each floor, each including generous terraces and inventive courtyards. Next to the CB29 Apartments is the more minimal and orthodox development from the "House on the Slope": the Miesian minimal units at Calle Calderon de la Barca 30 (2003-06), an exercise in the reduction of architecture to the slimmest and most elegant dimensions possible. At Calle Michelet 50 (2009-10), Dellekamp reworks the theme of the day-lit central stairway, forming a collective experience around which are gathered small studio-like units. Another refreshing typological solution is seen at the Calle Amsterdam 307 Apartments (2009-11) with loft-like linear units and saddleback service cores.

The CB29 Apartments are anything but Miesian, well, perhaps some of the minimal glazing detailing, and these only at a stretch, for Dellekamp is not tied to a Doric sensibility. The window glazing system is more like a minimal curtain. Behind this curtain are once again different layouts per floor. The suspected orthogonality is undercut by wedge spaces that on the one hand provide double-height volumes above living rooms for example and on the other hand create removed spaces, niches, or internalized bay windows. With this device, the apartment actually becomes more versatile than had it be formed of straightforward orthogonal box-like rooms.

The typology of the three CB29 Apartments is worth noting: here, each unit has a linear stair leading from the main apartment to an additional one bedroom or two bedrooms on the floor above. Thus, the "intrusion" of the wedges are not off-the-cuff gestures, but counterbalance the continuity of each apartment one level further up. Typologically then, the CB29 Apartments are an intelligent, inner-city development of the "House on the Slope", in fact, even though the site of the CB29 Apartment is more restrictive, Dellekamp has here created a more diverse and richer spatial experience than in the case of the free-standing house.

Tatiana Bilbao's Ajijic House and Derek Dellekamp's CB29 Apartments do not appear as if they are conceptually related. And yet, in tracing their architectural relatives, the two buildings reveal their underlying connections. Both are firmly rooted in their urban or landscape context, both are closely engaged in their respective sites, both derive diversity and richness from the juxtaposition of the basic orthogonal grain against diagonal, wedge like spaces. Both use opening or double-height gestures to expand the inhabitant's spatial experiences. Both demonstrate that there is a future for modern architecture, if only it frees itself from the simplistic dogma of its forefathers and pays closer attention to the reality on the ground.

Ajijic House, 2009 - 2011

Tatiana Bilbao

Ajijic House

Tatiana Bilbao

This weekend house, located on the shore of Chapala Lake in the state of Jalisco, just outside of the city of Guadalajara, was designed for a family with one daughter. In our imagination, this will be the house in which more than one member of the family will spend their last part of their lives.

We created a dual system to work on this site: firstly, a sense of a system that would enhance the relationship between the house and the landscape; secondly, and perhaps more importantly, a sense of a system between the site and the life of the family.

For this dual system, the complex spatial relationship between 4 cubes provides the inspiration. Two cubes are orientated towards the lake and the other two towards the town of Ajijic.

The cubes of the house represent both the single parts of the family, that is to say, the family made up of individuals, as well as the family as a complete unit.

The cubes provide possibilities for individual space, by partly touching, partly overlapping and partly connecting to each other. They create semi-public spaces in complex ways. They also allow the house to relate to the landscape and the interior in contrasting modes.

The siting of the house on the south-facing plot was defined by the overlapping of three different geometric traces of circles. The size of the circles was defined according to the most important sizes in the trace of the first sense of the dual system that we used to define the architecture, that is the cubes. By dividing the radius in two, a second trace of circle was defined; and similarly, the third trace was obtained by dividing the largest circle into three. While these circular traces and their fragments define the entire landscape around the house, it is essentially the relationships between the architecture, its interior and the site on the one hand, and the family and life on the other that are held by these traces.

We live in a society that values rapid consumption and complex reinvention while paradoxically searching for longevity, even immortality.
The family living in this house has reached its strengths of deeper and more coherent values on the basis of stability, well founded ethics, all of these nurtured by a lifelong exposure to art and architecture, a life of aesthetic relationships.

We needed a way to represent this in the designed spaces and forms, while at the same time we needed to find a low cost, low maintenance constructional system that would fit the client's budget. We needed a very gentle material that would provide a strong statement allowing us to play with different profound concepts, but also permitting us to play with a range of sensory qualities such as opacity, transparency and reflectivity of the inner spaces and the surroundings, simultaneously radiating this family's energies.

We decided to use one of the oldest and most enduring materials that exists in construction: compacted earth, a strong, direct material that would be the structure, the thermal insulation, and the aesthetic definition of the space all at the same time. Compacted earth complements the definition of the above system and traces while also being the point of intersection between them: the ground.

The use of this material allowed us to be consistent with the clients' desire to be in an open space with both relationships to the immediate surroundings as well as distant views, but also to have as much privacy in the intimate spaces as possible. We used the geometric definitions and the gestures of the roofs to underline these relationships. Two of the four cubes, those facing the lake, contain the more public areas such as the living and dinning rooms while the other one accommodates the private areas, bedrooms, bathrooms and the studio. The two other cubes link the two major domains while also becoming the entrance hall and the patio-terrace. These two spaces invoke the idea of human life in a habitat that is on the one hand coherent with our times, but on the other hand perhaps reticent towards other external conditions.

The traces of circles and squares are used to define all constructions above 15 cm of the ground. Thus, for the caretaker's house, we used the same geometric system to build their house and garage.

The circles define floor finishes and landscape elements, everything 'below' 15 cm to the ground, allowing us to define the disposition of the vegetable and herb garden including the orchard and other native plants. We redefined some relationships between the house and the site, blocking some or allowing other views, but we also treated each part of the site according to its orientation and sun exposure.
Our practice likes to collaborate with people of other disciplines to help develop each project. We believe that an architecture responding to contemporary life has to be produced with a conjunction of minds educated in different disciplines. In order to enhance the experience and language of the house, we realized that we needed to work with different artists to make interventions and interpretations of the spaces. Thinking of the life of the family, we were certain that we needed wider associations to extend this life into the spatial experience. For this purpose, we thought we would work with one group of artists that would reinterpret this spatial experience into a single expression of art.

We invited Rodolfo Diaz and Marco Rountree, two young artists from Mexico City to work on the bathrooms. Their idea works with the design of the house, using once again a 'system' to produce specific bathroom tiles. Diaz and Rountree chose 10 x 10 white ceramic tiles and had them painted in two different ways, both in light pink. The combination of the two different tile types created entirely different surface patterns for all the areas in the house that had to be tiled. So as not to block the relationship with the landscape, but still guarding the privacy of bathrooms and changing rooms, we commissioned another young artist form Guadalajara, Cynthia Gutierrez, to develop a 'filter' that would let light in and provide views of the landscape, while at the same time blocking the views of the inside. She reinterpreted the surroundings with graphic and geometric lines, cutting layers of vinyl that are assembled into screens and placed in front of the windows.

The involvement of the client within the design and the construction was key for its development; amongst us, we generated a bond during the design and building process of this house, from the paper design phase onwards. This bond was such, that, half way into the construction phase, the client started to design her own furniture, something she had never done before, and the respective piece is now part of the house.

The design of light fittings is truly simple, and the only lamps that we incorporated were six specifically designed pieces for this house by the well-known Cuban artist Jorge Pardo.
Every part of this house supersedes the idea of globalism in preference for localism, a localism that is closer to a sense of individuality. We are living in post-humanist times, but this house insists on neither ignoring the need for human relationships with the surroundings nor the need for an ethical relationship to life.

View from the lake

Tatiana Bilbao's Casa Ajijic at Lake Chapala
Patrick Charpenel

At the dawn of the last century, a generation of visionary architects in the Mexican state of Jalisco—christened the Tapatía School of Architecture—burst on the scene. Each of these creators—who first captured the public's attention as a group in the 1930s—achieved notable professional solidity by marking out the lineaments of a wholly regional constructive style. Reviving certain techniques and materials previously used for ranch and hacienda construction in the west of Mexico, and highlighting historic Moorish styles prominent during the nation's viceregal period, Luis Barragán, Pedro Castellanos, Ignacio Díaz Morales and Rafael Urzúa created an architecture that was at the same time traditional and avant-garde.

Members of the Tapatía School erected magnificent works, in key sites in and around Guadalajara, in the school's characteristic vernacular style. One such case is Lake Chapala (in Nahautl, the language of the Aztecs, chapala means "place of the urns"), Mexico's largest lake in terms of water volume. In this oneiric Eden, the four Tapatío architects produced exceptional architecture that in one way or another knew precisely how to respond to their sites' natural, cultural and visual conditions.

Vast and elongated, Lake Chapala lies 50 km to the south of Mexico's "second city," Guadalajara, and features a surface area of 1112 m2 along with 8,000,000,000 m3 of water. Both in form and dimension, Lake Chapala is considered one of the most impressive sites in all western Mexico; numerous families in communities lining the lake have built country houses there as a means of getting away from it all or admiring its sumptuous landscape.

In the twenty-first century, and in view of the acceleration that electricity and its derivative technologies have wrought, the creation of "resistance zones" that reduce the speed of human experience—that let us reencounter spiritual spaces and moments—is essential. The economic development large European, Asian and American urban centers have achieved, and, in recent decades, the advancement of certain scientific and cultural expressions, has come with social benefits felt across enormous portions of the planet, but at the same time has been responsible for a saturation of cheap goods and worldwide ecological degradation. Numerous political organizations and economic structures have confronted this panorama and this has directly influenced life conditions for women and men of recent generations.

The notion of cultural identity (along with all its essentialist baggage) no longer fits into this contemporary paradigm and has given way to an idea of "context" from which the question of each place's specific conditions is posited, call these conditions what you will: cultural traditions, the politics of power, social psychology or the environmental problems that affect every area. So it is therefore worthwhile to examine young Mexican architect Tatiana Bilbao's constructive perspectives and architectural practice as they respond to each region's particular conditions, and always in consideration of their environments' specific elements.

Tatiana Bilbao imagined Casa Ajijic by taking up those same moral principles and applying them to a unique architectural expression. The estate is located in the town of Jocotepec, a small community on the edge of its grand, natural lake, in an area inhabited by fishermen, farmers and ranchers of Toltec origin. Construction work on the house began in 2010, using materials native to the arid soils of Mexico's western region: compacted clay of different tonalities that bind landmass to lake-scape.

From her earliest constructions, Bilbao has been concerned with an integration of structure into the natural contours of every surface. It was for that reason she was invited to develop a master structures and paths plan for Culiacán, Sinaloa's Botanical Garden in 2007. It took inspiration from the branching patterns observed in the park's trees and led to broken forms that connect to Sinaloa's exuberant plant life. Simultaneously, concrete construction references the region's rocks and boulders and creates an effect of visual contrast. Casa Ajijic recaptures the same constructive philosophy, artfully blending and clashing with elements that form its universe.

Conceived for a family of three adults, the house presents generous and flexible spaces within a relatively restricted surface area. Two thousand square meters in extension, the lot situates a country estate at a strategic point from which its different material components are masterfully distributed. Inspired by a number of glass pavilions produced by renowned American conceptual artist Dan Graham (b. Urbana, Illinois, 1942), the house evinces the lines of a symmetrical inverse geometry that recalls the Chinese yin and yang device. The house underscores its strong connection to the conceptual artist and additionally integrates art objects by other contemporary creators such as Jalisco's Cynthia Gutiérrez, Cuban artist Jorge Pardo, Englishman Liam Gillick, Carol Bove of Switzerland and Germany's Mathias Goeritz. The rectilinear structure creates something of an angular mirror that produces a beautiful replica superimposed at its other extreme.

The structure occupies 300 m2 on two levels and its walls portray pigments in a series of layers that generate an approximately 1.7 m visual horizon. This dimension rises the scale of a person and affords the house a more human proportion. The

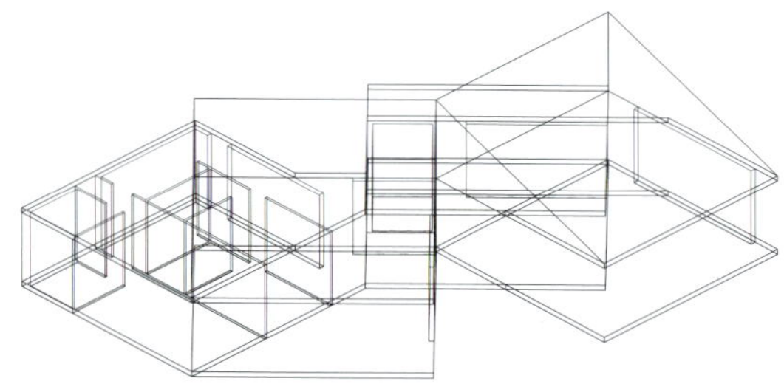

Isometric drawing of Ajijic House

Dan Graham, Münster Pavilion, 1987

caretaker's cottage and the garage—as if on a small island—are found at the estate's northern perimeter. The structure of the main house rises from two compounds that meet in a central area, creating an intersection that serves as a connector for two general floor plans, and links the first section's bedrooms and studio to the living area and kitchen in the second.

As a complement to the house's space distribution, the southern sides of the bedrooms and living area feature large picture windows that frame the lake's waters beautifully and open on to two terraces that extend to the garden. The form of this visual horizon is accentuated by the presence of pitched ceilings at open angles that play drastically with overhead space, allowing for the introduction of an even higher level: the studio and library. The lower platform features a white terrazzo disk that contrasts with wood flooring running horizontally until it reaches outdoor space. In a way, the clash between the house's rectangular form and the floor's circumferential design produces rhythm, accent and contrast.

Elsewhere, an extensive Pennisetum-grass garden that covers the entire outdoor space reminds us that Chapala's fine weather is the consequence of a hydraulic depression that unites the Lerma and Santiago Rivers. Because of these geographic conditions, the Lake enjoys a temperate, highly pleasant climate where one finds varied vegetation featuring tule, ahuehuete, and willow trees, along with subtropical scrub species such as copales, pepelillo, huizache, huamúchil and zapote, as well as fertile topsoil fit for chayote and maize cultivation. In response to the ecosystem's sylvan beauty, Casa Ajijic boasts it own orchard—its private natural microcosm—whose produce is reserved for the exclusive consumption of the estate's three permanent residents.

Yin and Yang symbolism speaks to a dualist distribution of forces made up of an active and passive principle contained within a ring divided along a sigmoid curve. The emblem's design creates two fields that link opposing worlds (a world of total darkness and a world of light) to produce a figure in constant, antipodal movement. The center of the sign serves as the sole escape from this great whirlwind and the compound's symmetry is the culmination of perfect balance, where the placement of each component part functions in perfect relation to the aggregate whole. It justifies Casa Ajijic's evocation of the Asiatic, which guarantees harmony, correct proportions and an unwavering mensurability throughout the constructed work. Thus Casa Ajijic is a complex that integrates the natural and the artificial—the external and the internal—in a dynamic, structural form.

If nature and humankind must respond to ecological and economic problems that assail them, then they must also operate from new conceptual or methodological platforms. Tatiana Bilbao has devised multiple urban and architectural projects in this mode, perennially responding to the specific conditions of each context and culture. Her office has developed technical strategies that satisfy user or client requirements yet simultaneously recognize and make us sensible to the intrinsic values of every project.

Considered from this perspective, Bilbao recaptures the work habits each of Jalisco's four modern architects cultivated, since, like them, she gathers local elements and improves the space's environmental conditions. At the same time she studies the social dynamics of those who use and inhabit the territory into which she inserts every project. If globalism has yet to follow a uniform expansion process ordered entirely by economic imperatives, it is because it must still recognize the disjunctive flow of cultural, information and political landscapes. This can mean that globalization carries with it dynamic movement that is not ordered by any rectifying plan, but rather is fractured and disconnected as a function of its speed.

Casa Ajijic, located in a community whose population now reaches 38,000, is a product that understands the cultural practices of the surrounding inhabitants; a magical refuge that respects the topography of this irregular plain; a locus that responds to the lake's climatic conditions; and above all a structure that incorporates Chapala's light, vistas, time and space. As a consequence of its structure of materials and constructive design, the adobe walls regulates interior temperatures; rooflines play capriciously with mountain ridges and the water's infinite horizontality; multiple circular plantings (executed in collaboration with Mexico City's Taller de Operaciones Ambientales workshop) showcase western Mexico's endemic flora.

If the Chapala Riviera was the birthplace of large-scale architectural projects at the end of the nineteenth century, and if it has known how to conserve both its calm and the vitality of its peaceful residents, then it is the responsibility of its people to create infrastructure that strengthens the region's economic dynamic. And at the same time, it is everyone's responsibility to regenerate the ecosystem the lies inside the lake and within the volcanic cones and domes that surround it. Tatiana Bilbao makes a positive impact within the site's context precisely for these reasons.

Our original premise affirmed that contemporary architecture must re-posit its purpose in response to the demands of a globalized culture. Assuming that this discipline can take each site and context's particularities into consideration, we can conclude that the architecture of the future must produce works that in each case bring together the values of an interconnected world and, at the same time, respond to each space or place's needs. Casa Ajijic, here in the State of Jalisco, Mexico, is the prototype for these new structural models.

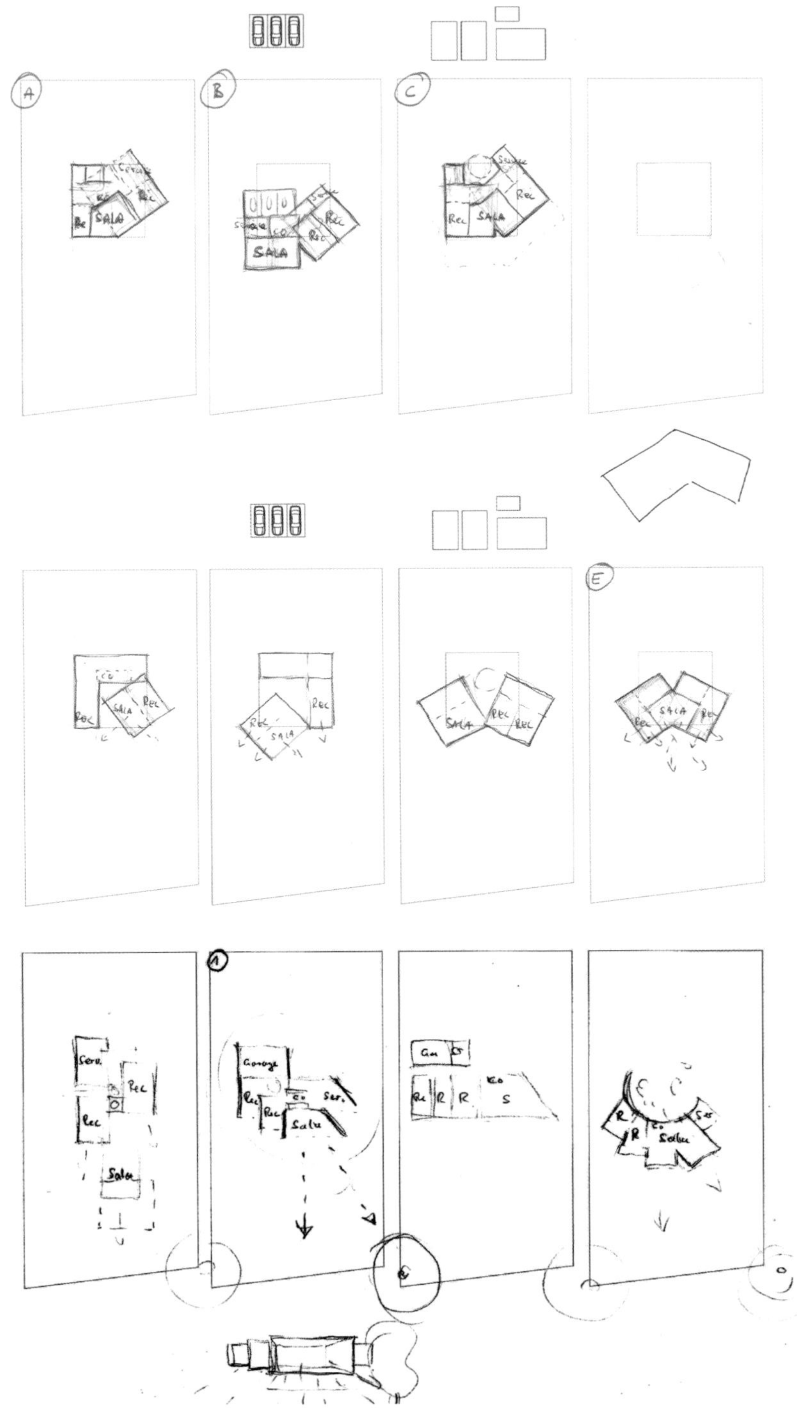

Above and Opposite: Conceptual Investigation sketches

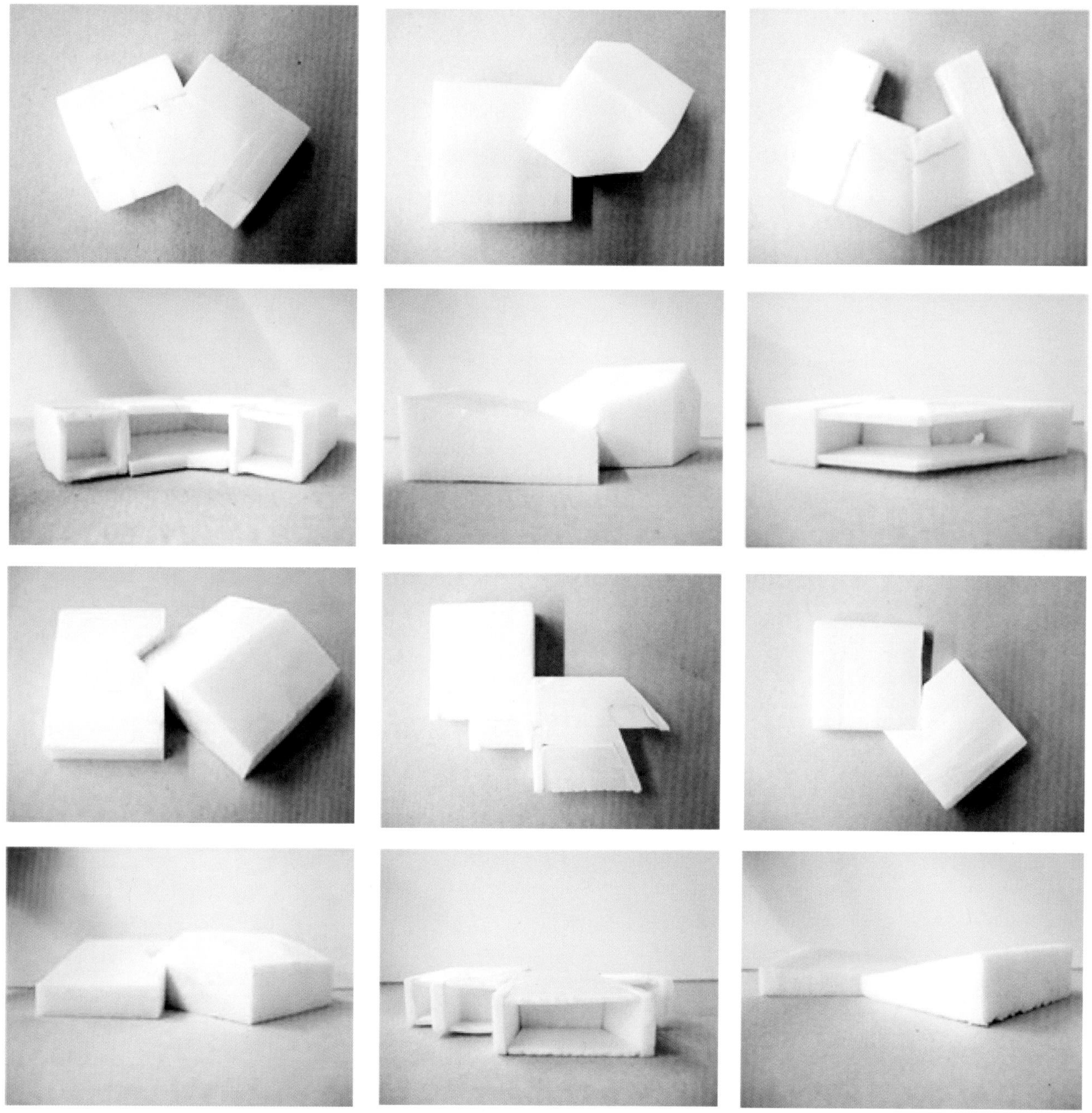

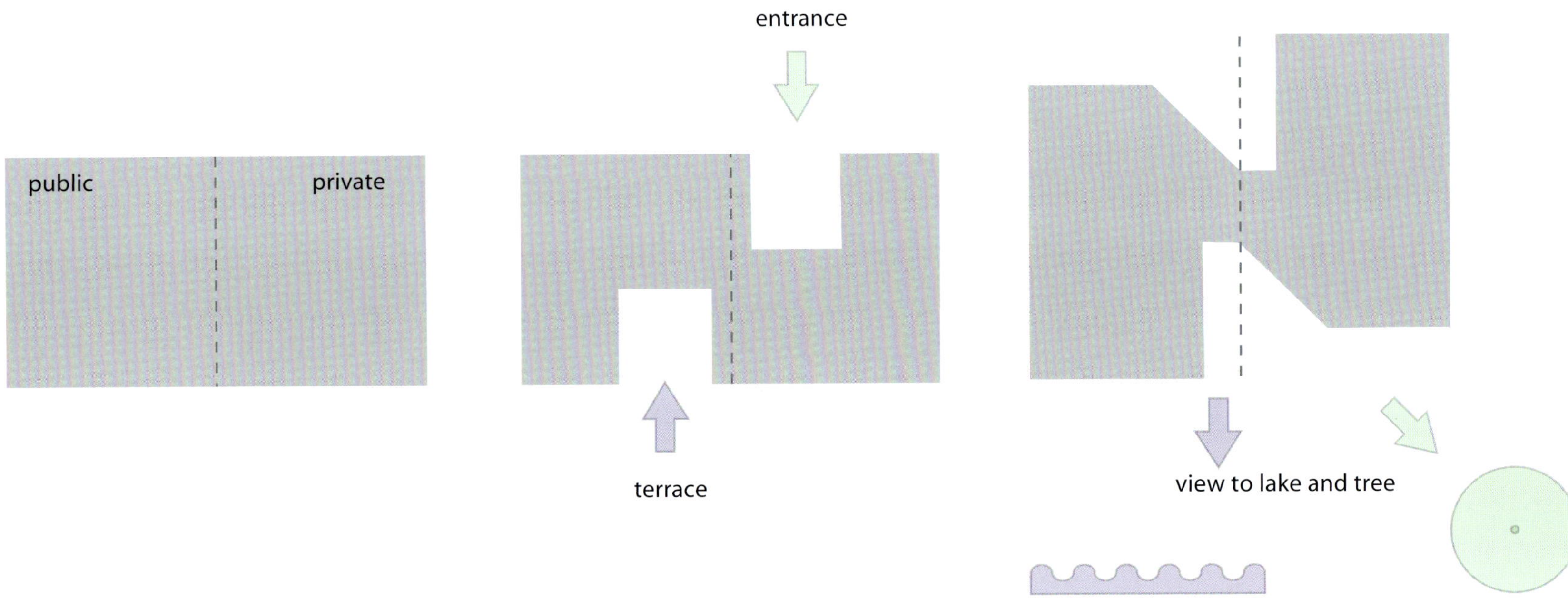

Above and Opposite: Conceptual Scheme

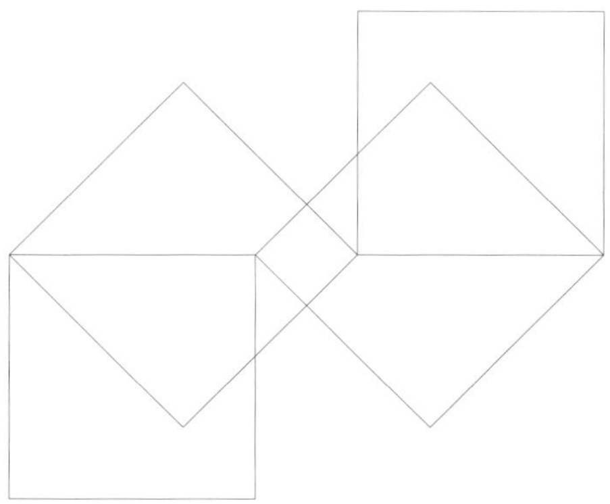

trace

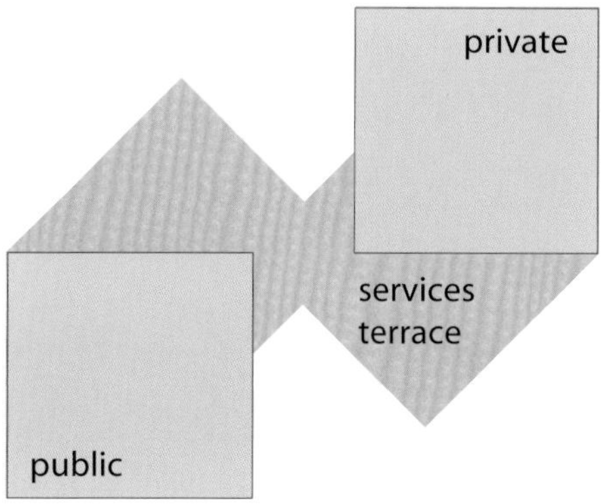

volume

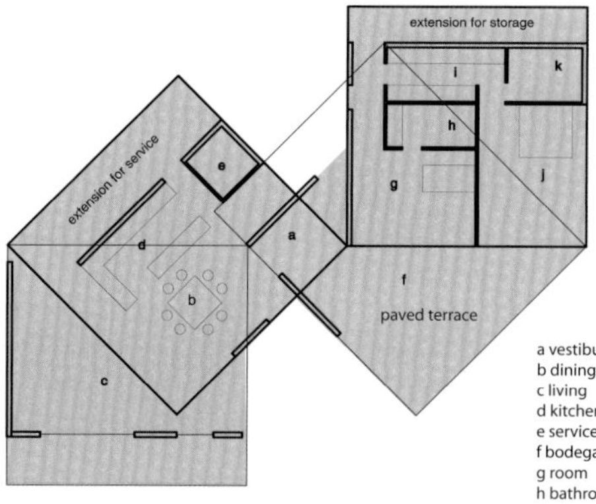

walls

a vestibule
b dining
c living
d kitchen
e services/wc
f bodega
g room
h bathroom
i locker
j master bedroom
k bathroom

Above: Intersection Model
Opposite: Roof Studies

Above and Opposite: Conceptual Earth Models

Above: Interior Studies
Opposite: Material Studies

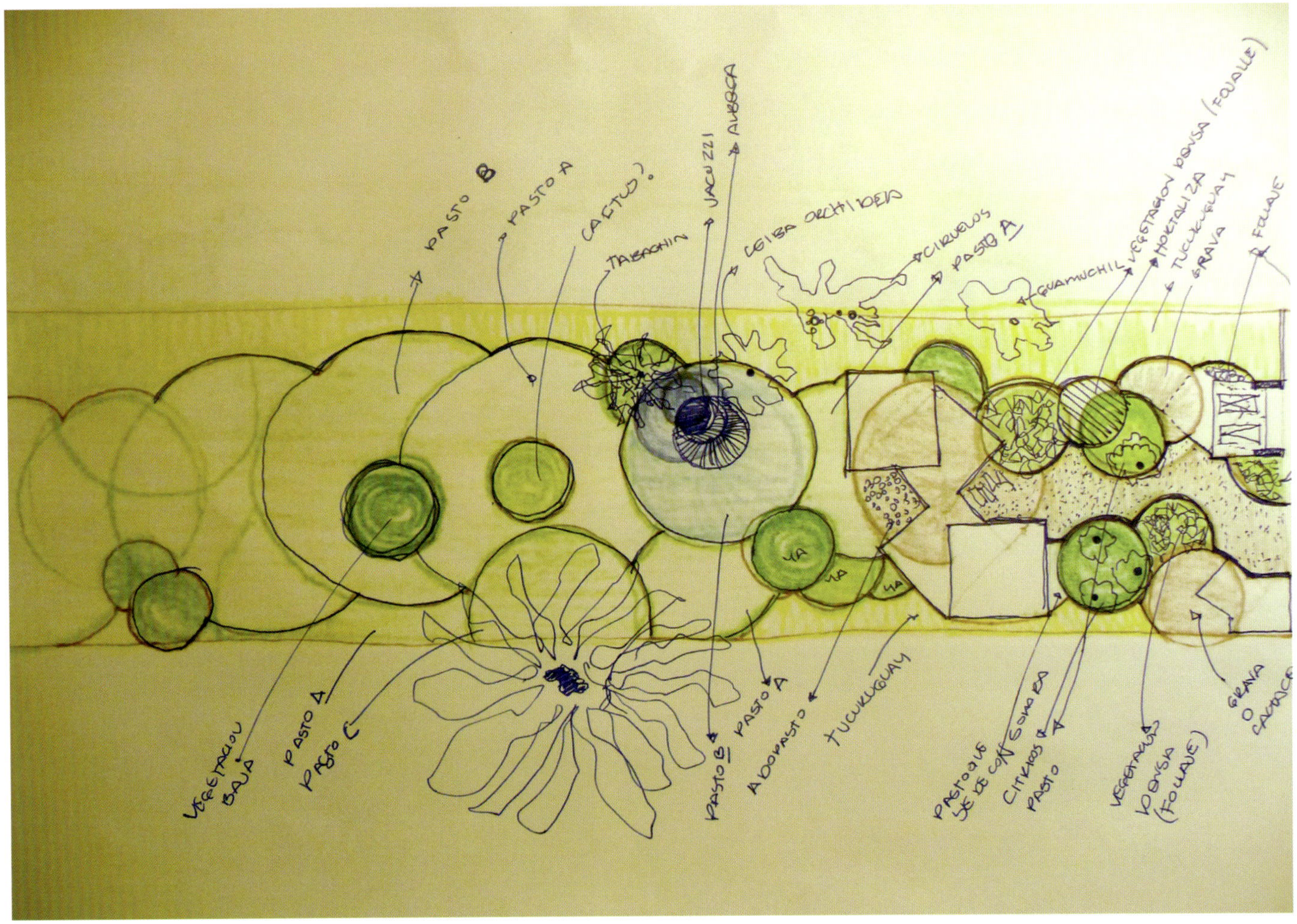

Above and Opposite: Landscape Concept

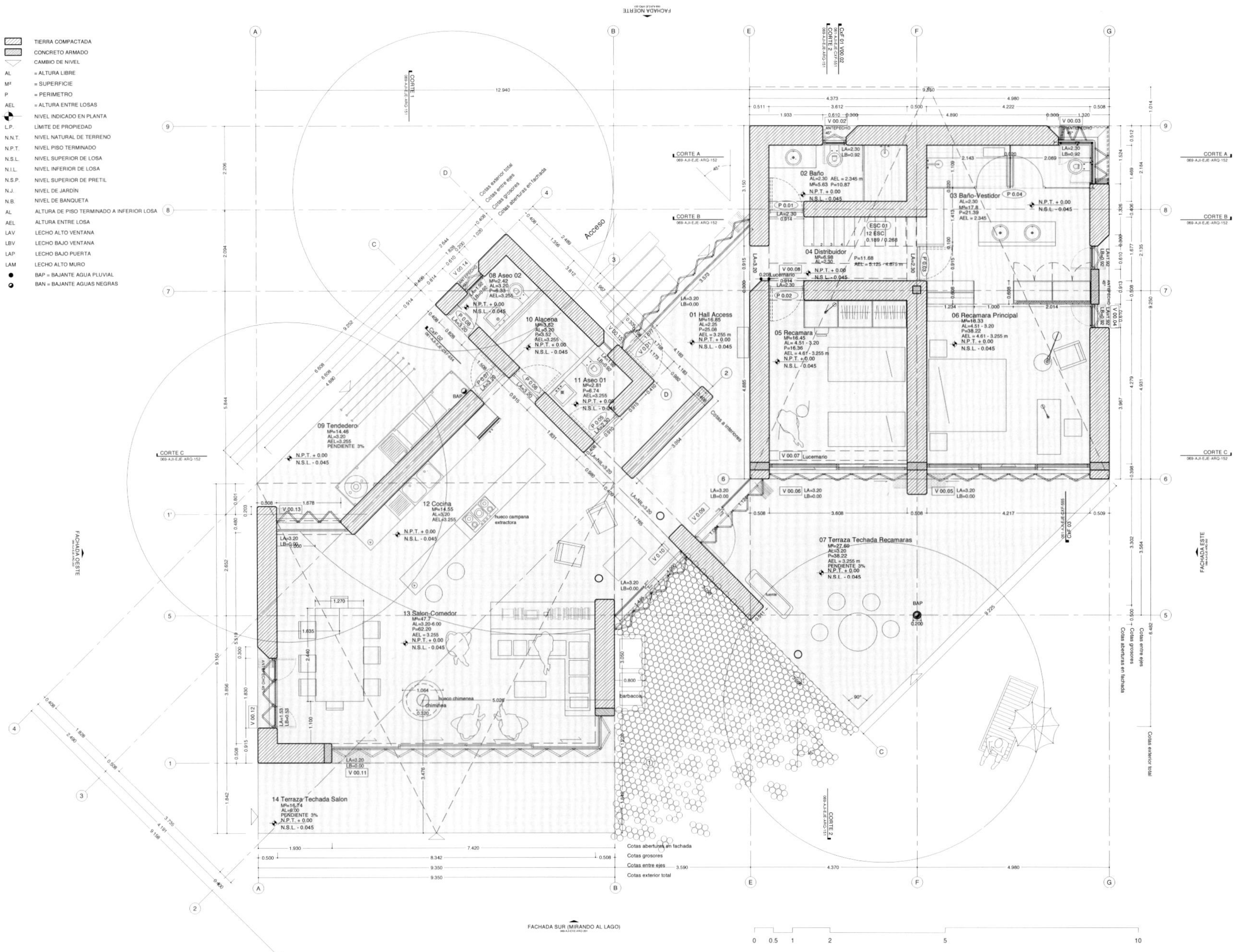
FACHADA NORTE
TIERRA COMPACTADA
CONCRETO ARMADO
CAMBIO DE NIVEL
AL = ALTURA LIBRE
M² = SUPERFICIE
P = PERIMETRO
AEL = ALTURA ENTRE LOSAS
NIVEL INDICADO EN PLANTA
L.P. LÍMITE DE PROPIEDAD
N.N.T. NIVEL NATURAL DE TERRENO
N.P.T. NIVEL PISO TERMINADO
N.S.L. NIVEL SUPERIOR DE LOSA
N.I.L. NIVEL INFERIOR DE LOSA
N.S.P. NIVEL SUPERIOR DE PRETIL
N.J. NIVEL DE JARDÍN
N.B. NIVEL DE BANQUETA
AL ALTURA DE PISO TERMINADO A INFERIOR LOSA
AEL ALTURA ENTRE LOSAS
LAV LECHO ALTO VENTANA
LBV LECHO BAJO VENTANA
LAP LECHO BAJO PUERTA
LAM LECHO ALTO MURO
BAP = BAJANTE AGUA PLUVIAL
BAN = BAJANTE AGUAS NEGRAS
Acceso
01 Hall Access
02 Baño
03 Baño-Vestidor
04 Distribuidor
05 Recamara
06 Recamara Principal
07 Terraza Techada Recamaras
08 Aseo 02
09 Tendedero
10 Alacena
11 Aseo 01
12 Cocina
13 Salon-Comedor
14 Terraza Techada Salon
hueco campana extractora
hueco chimenea
Chimenea
Barbacoa
Lucernario
FACHADA OESTE
FACHADA ESTE
FACHADA SUR (MIRANDO AL LAGO)
CORTE A
CORTE B
CORTE C
Cotas aberturas en fachada
Cotas grosores
Cotas entre ejes
Cotas exterior total
0 0.5 1 2 5 10

O'NF

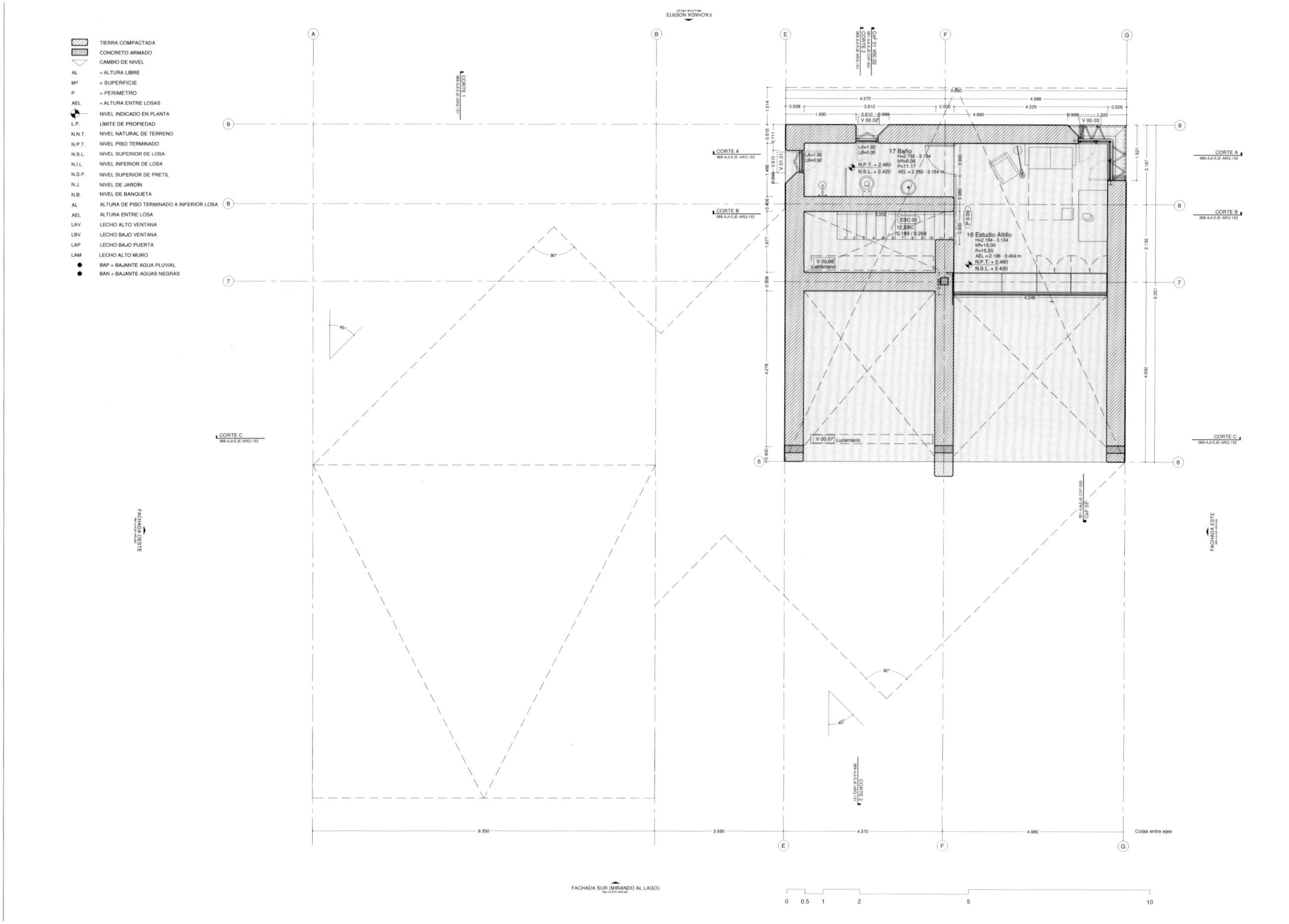
TIERRA COMPACTADA
CONCRETO ARMADO
CAMBIO DE NIVEL
AL = ALTURA LIBRE
M² = SUPERFICIE
P = PERIMETRO
AEL = ALTURA ENTRE LOSAS
NIVEL INDICADO EN PLANTA
L.P. LÍMITE DE PROPIEDAD
N.N.T. NIVEL NATURAL DE TERRENO
N.P.T. NIVEL PISO TERMINADO
N.S.L. NIVEL SUPERIOR DE LOSA
N.I.L. NIVEL INFERIOR DE LOSA
N.S.P. NIVEL SUPERIOR DE PRETIL
N.J. NIVEL DE JARDÍN
N.B. NIVEL DE BANQUETA
AL ALTURA DE PISO TERMINADO A INFERIOR LOSA
AEL ALTURA ENTRE LOSA
LAV LECHO ALTO VENTANA
LBV LECHO BAJO VENTANA
LAP LECHO BAJO PUERTA
LAM LECHO ALTO MURO
BAP = BAJANTE AGUA PLUVIAL
BAN = BAJANTE AGUAS NEGRAS
FACHADA NORTE
FACHADA OESTE
FACHADA ESTE
FACHADA SUR (MIRANDO AL LAGO)
CORTE A
CORTE B
CORTE C
17 Baño
16 Estudio Altillo
N.P.T. + 2.460
N.S.L. + 2.420
V 00.07 Lucernario
Cotas entre ejes
9.350
3.590
4.370
4.980
0 0.5 1 2 5 10

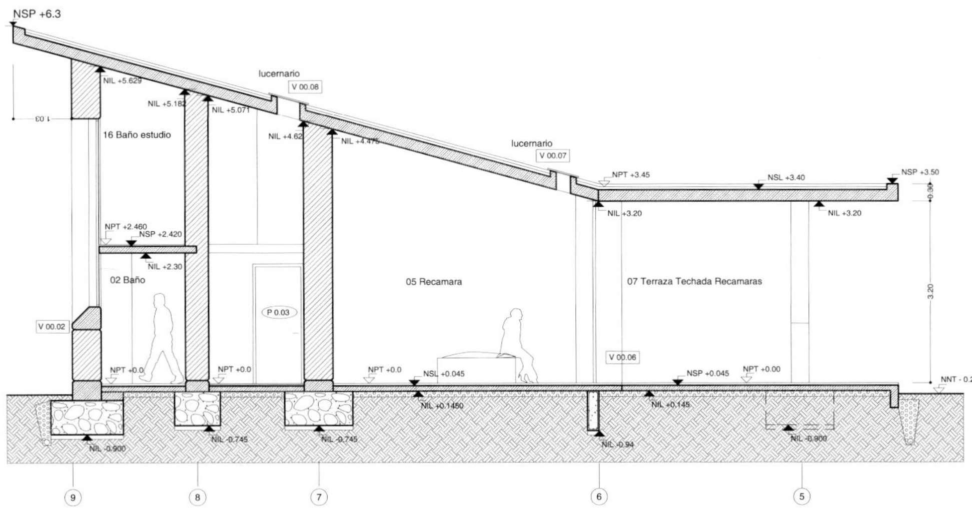

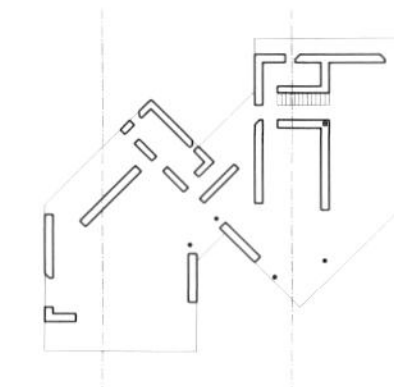

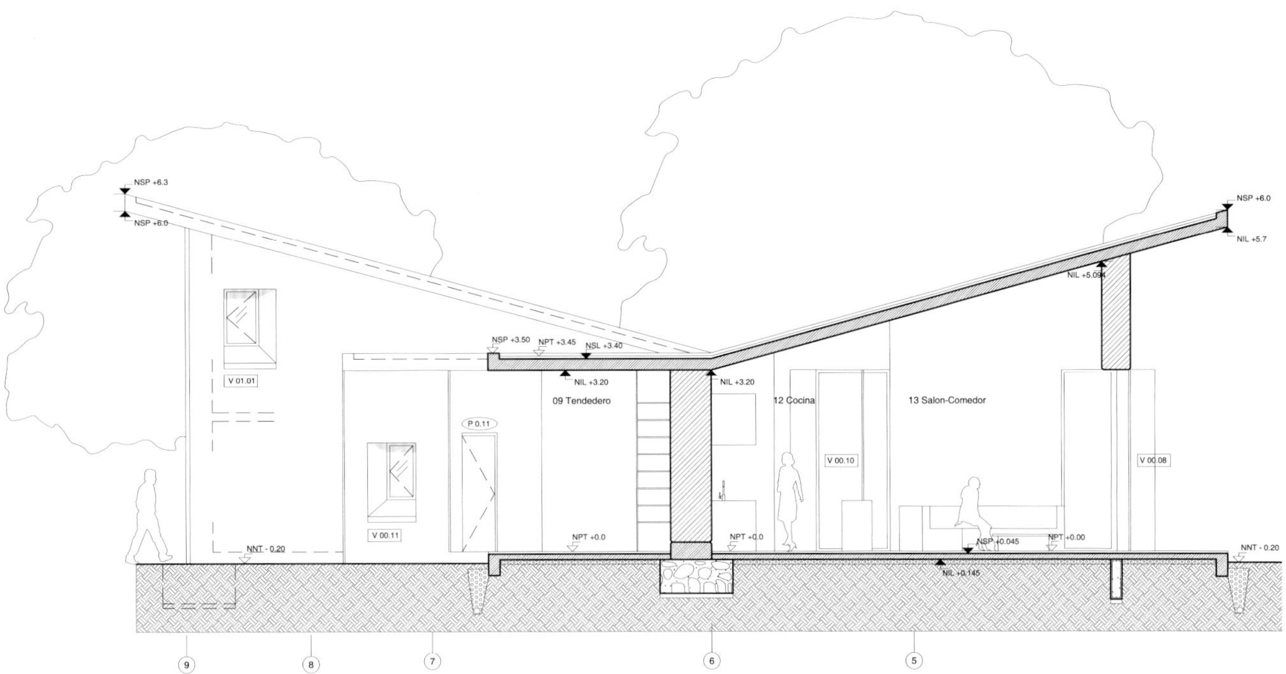

CORTE 1
089-AJI-EXE-ARQ-151

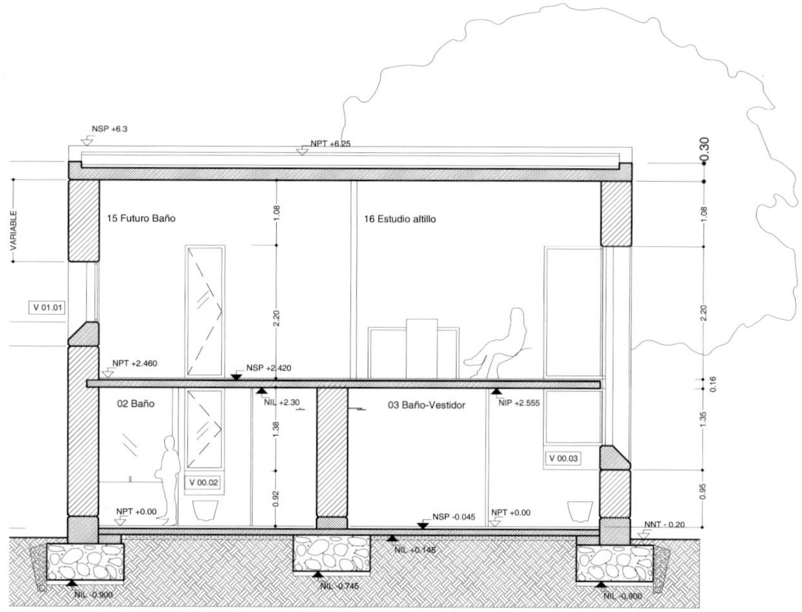

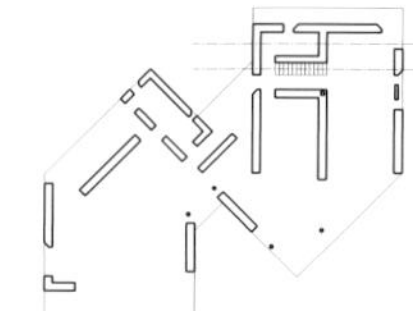

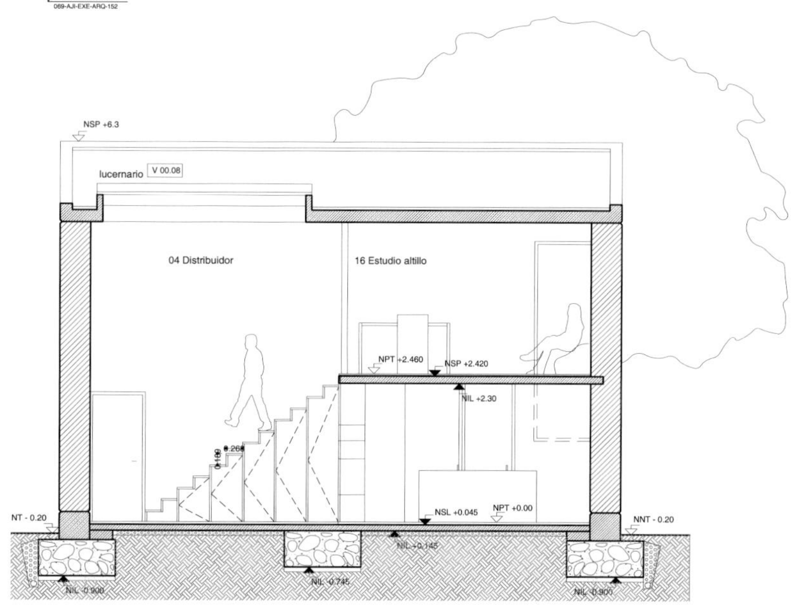

Opposite: Cross Sections 1 & 2
This Page: Cross Sections A & B

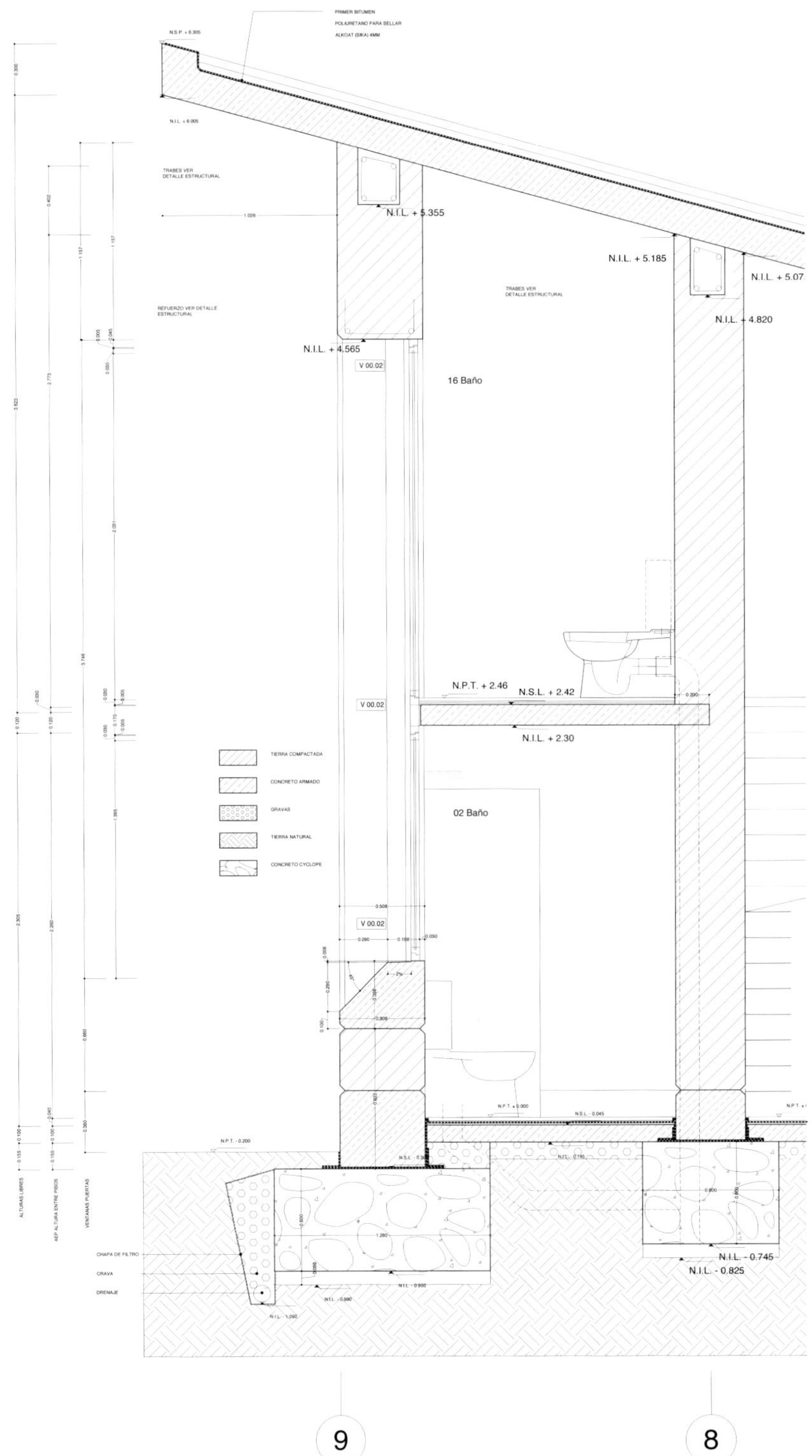
N.I.L. + 5.355
N.I.L. + 5.185
N.I.L. + 5.07
N.I.L. + 4.820
N.I.L. + 4.565
16 Baño
N.P.T. + 2.46
N.S.L. + 2.42
N.I.L. + 2.30
02 Baño
N.I.L. - 0.745
N.I.L. - 0.825
9
8
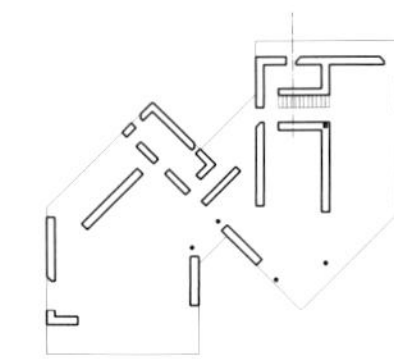

O'NFD

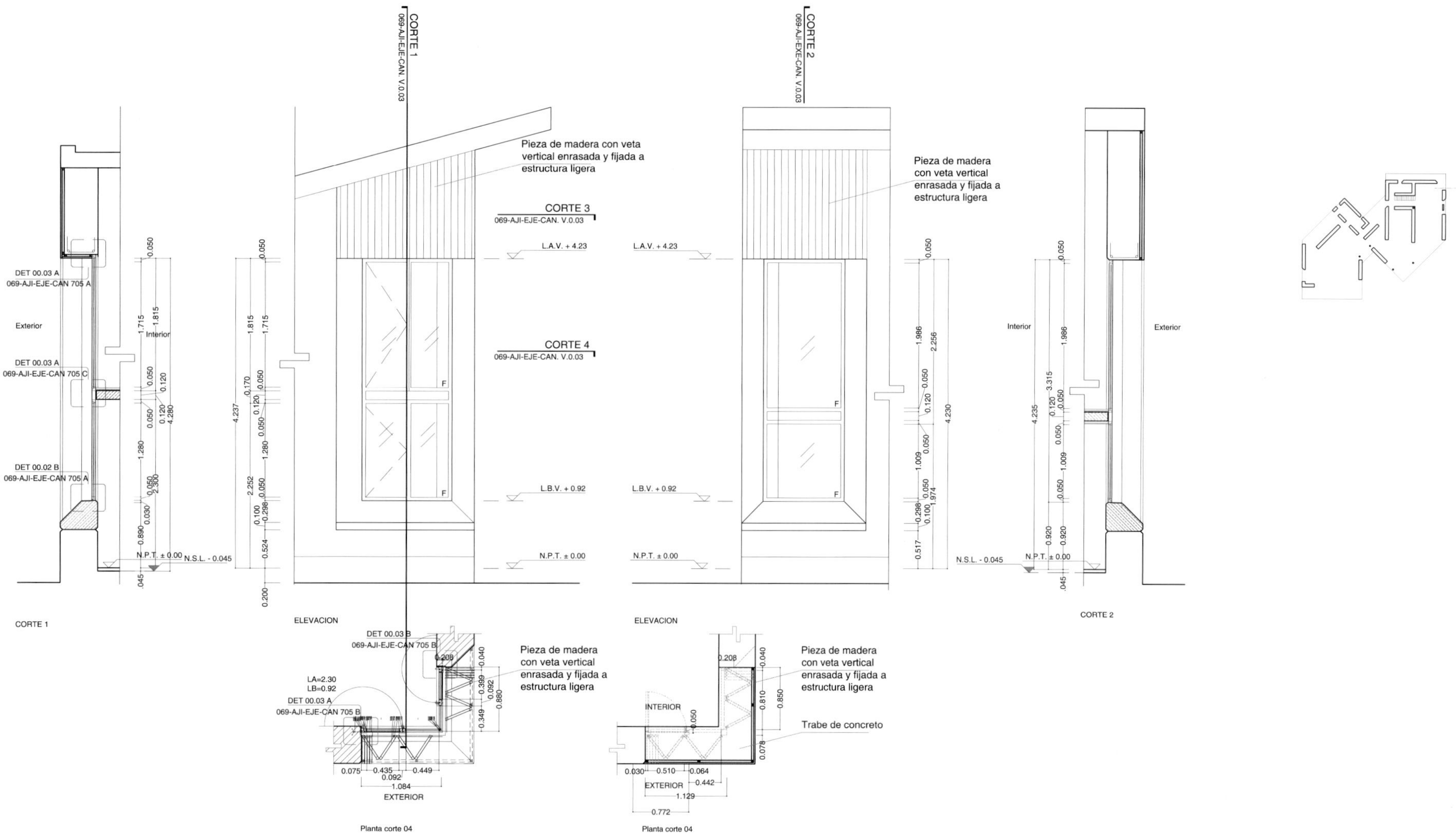
CORTE 1
069-AJI-EJE-CAN. V.0.03
CORTE 2
069-AJI-EXE-CAN. V.0.03
Pieza de madera con veta vertical enrasada y fijada a estructura ligera
CORTE 3
069-AJI-EJE-CAN. V.0.03
CORTE 4
069-AJI-EJE-CAN. V.0.03
L.A.V. + 4.23
L.B.V. + 0.92
N.P.T. ± 0.00
N.S.L. - 0.045
DET 00.03 A
069-AJI-EJE-CAN 705 A
Exterior
Interior
DET 00.03 A
069-AJI-EJE-CAN 705 C
DET 00.02 B
069-AJI-EJE-CAN 705 A
CORTE 1
ELEVACION
ELEVACION
CORTE 2
DET 00.03 B
069-AJI-EJE-CAN 705 B
LA=2.30
LB=0.92
DET 00.03 A
069-AJI-EJE-CAN 705 B
EXTERIOR
INTERIOR
Trabe de concreto
Planta corte 04
Planta corte 04

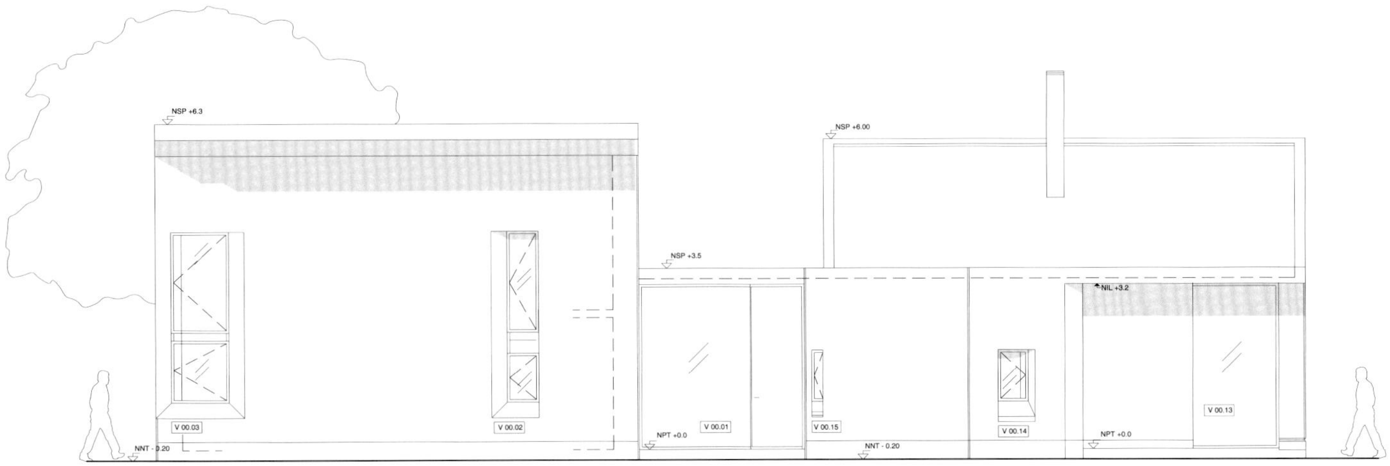

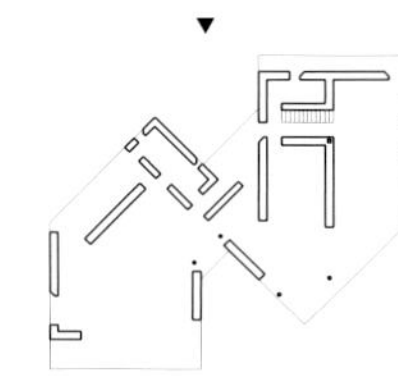

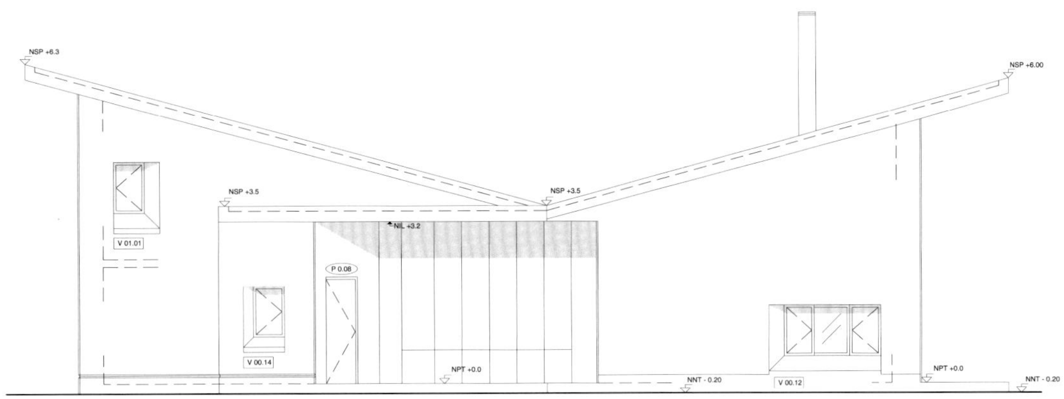

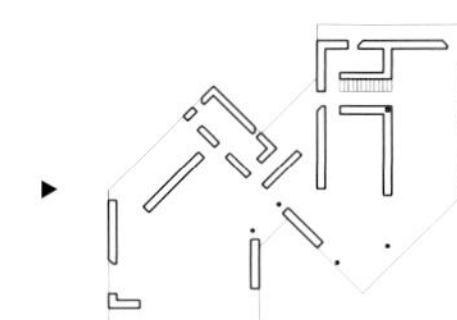

Top: North elevation.
Bottom: West elevation.

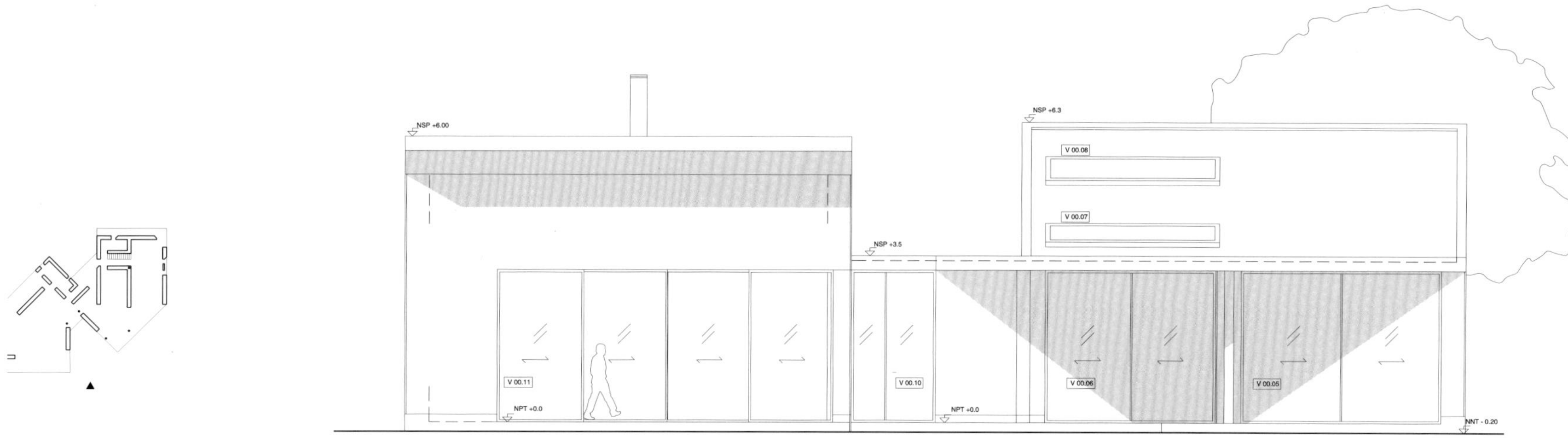

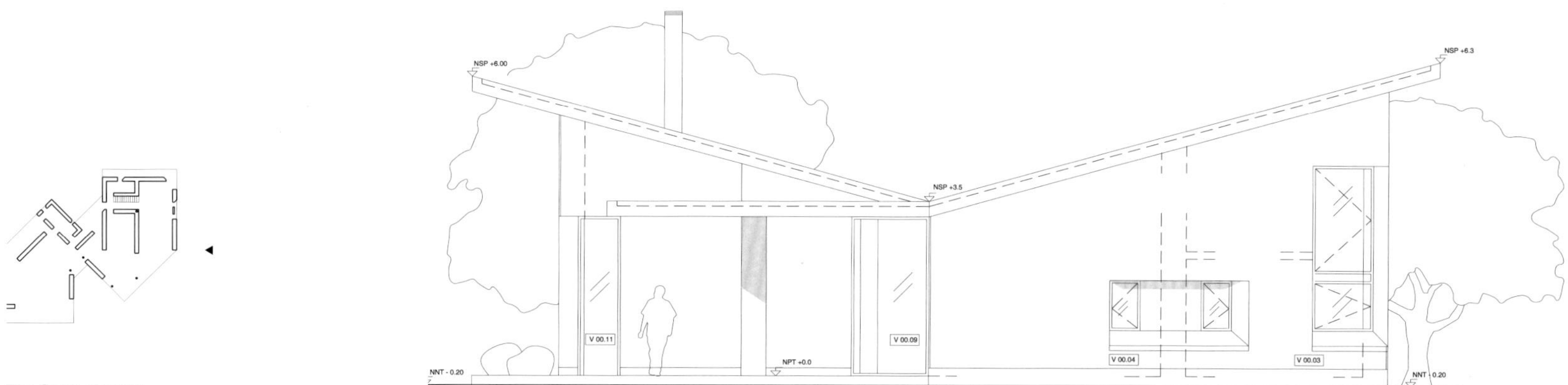

Top: South elevation.
Bottom: East elevation

Above and Opposite: Bathroom tile studies

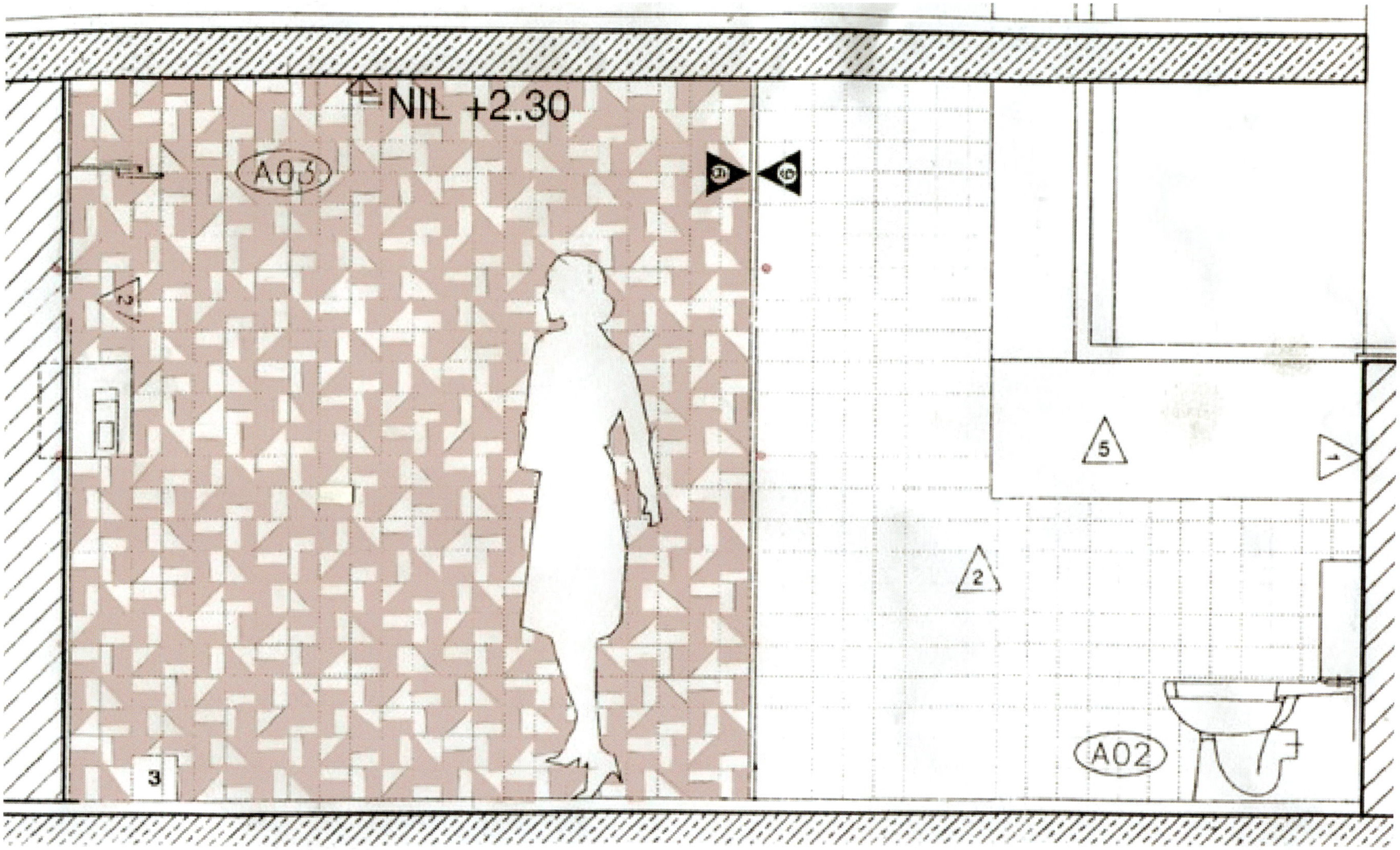
NIL +2.30
A03
2
3
5
1
2
A02

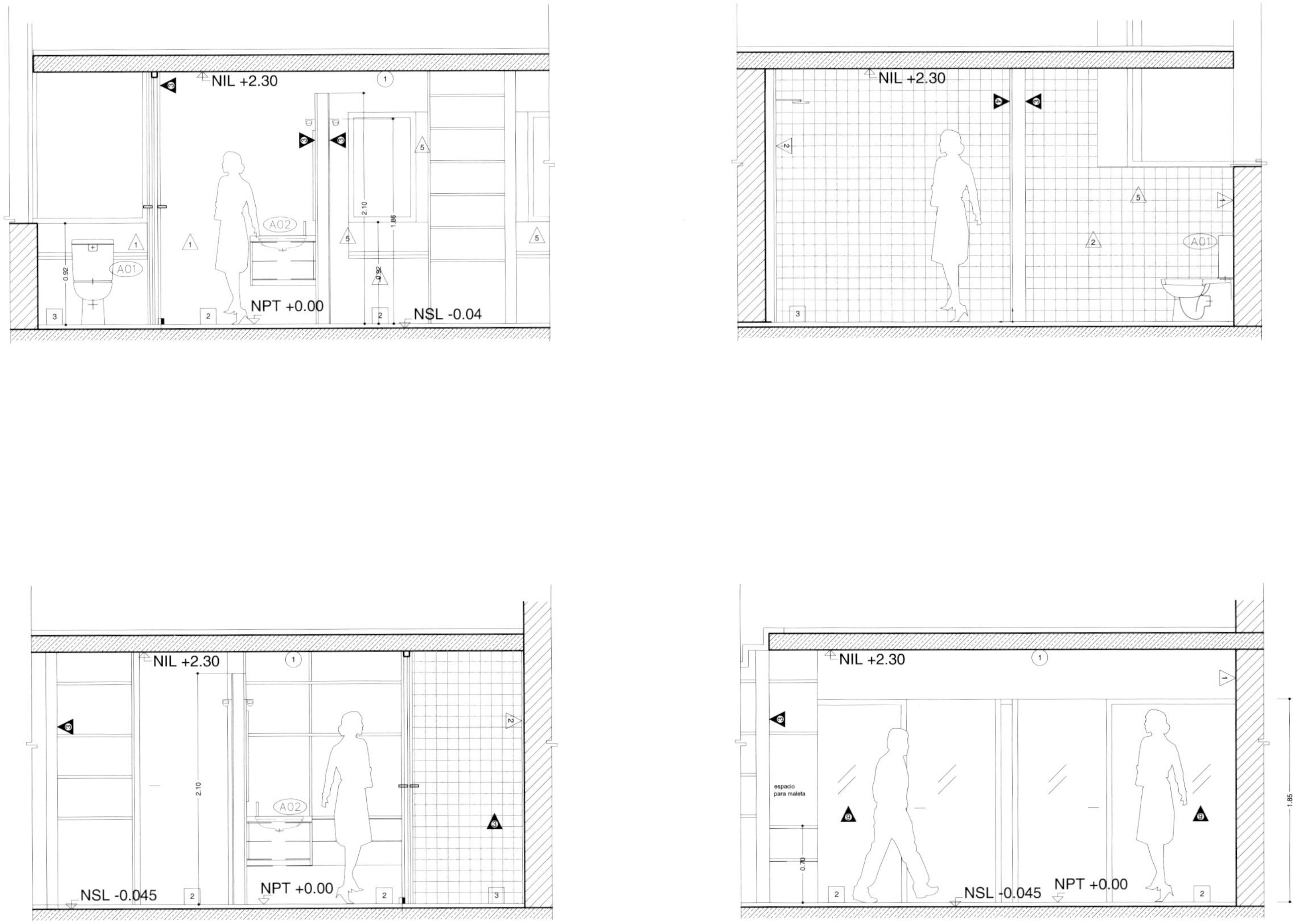

Window Details for First Floor and Upstairs.

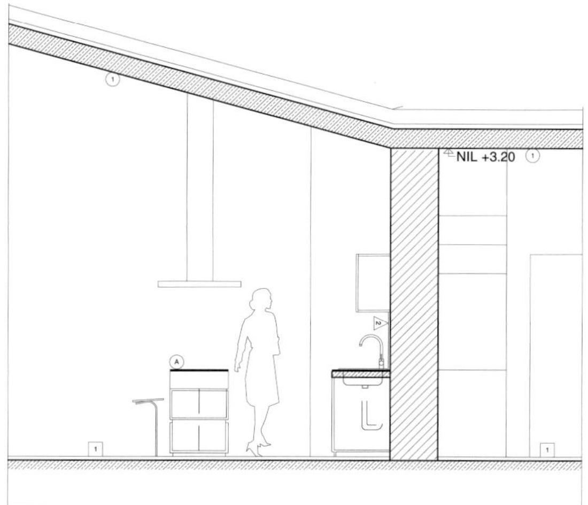
NIL +3.20

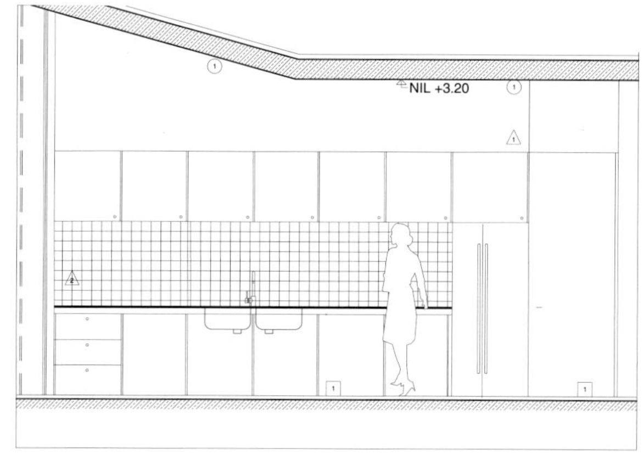
NIL +3.20

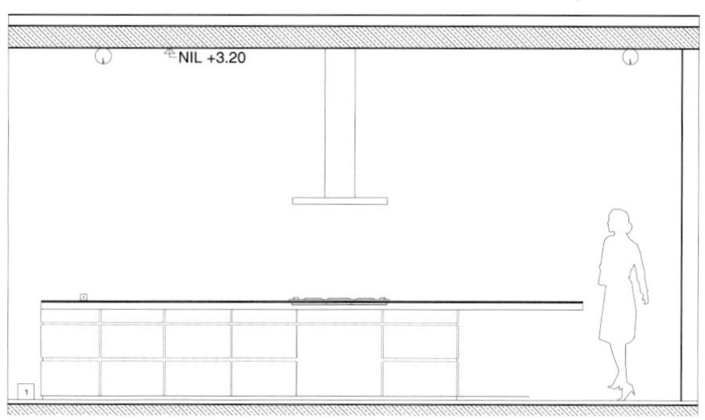
NIL +3.20

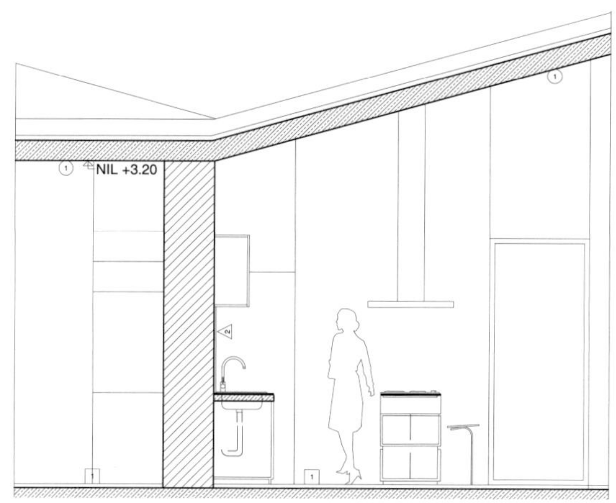
NIL +3.20

Above: Installed view protection for main entrance area
Opposite: Studies Protection for Windows

Construction Photos

Atlas Copco
XAS 97
185 CFM

CB29 Apartments, 2005 – 2007

Dellekamp Arquitectos

Essay

The Construction of a System

Fernanda Canales

In the late 1990s, when Derek Dellekamp began his career, Mexico City was undergoing an important change. Despite all catastrophic predictions of a city that had doubled its number of inhabitants each decade throughout the 20th century, the capital had not reached even half the population mark announced for the early 21st. Leaving behind the category of a paralyzing city landscape, a new age of optimism and change infused Dellekamp's generation. The capital, which Time Magazine had proclaimed as the "worst-case scenario of cities" in 1984, became for the younger generation a normal place that not only ceased to press with fatalistic forecasts, but began to represent a landscape of great potential.

Following the arrival of democracy in the year 2000 and the overcoming of the 1994 economic crisis, the new millennium dawned on a city of new projects. Mexico City became for the new generation of architects an experimental laboratory full of possibilities. The re-densification of central areas was implemented as a strategy to modify the city's urban sprawl growing unevenly towards suburbia. Dellekamp's first work, an apartment building in Alfonso Reyes Avenue (2003) in Colonia Condesa, represented the climax of a wave of interventions in a neighborhood that had become rather obsolete after the earthquake in 1985, and was the new fashionable place to live, a mecca of design and urban living.

Since his first project, Dellekamp´s work is based in the redefinition of dwelling space, re-thinking the architect's position regarding given solutions, where often only formal aspects are considered. The re-densification process undergone in Mexico City during the first decade of the 21st century that had generated a proliferation of apartment buildings – first in Colonia Condesa and later in the neighborhoods of Polanco, Anzures and Roma – consisted of new developments that were almost exclusively the repetition of a single architectural formula and layout, which reduced the job to little more than an attractive façade-design fitted into the constraints of the extant buildings' party walls. For Dellekamp, however, each of his projects in this line– Calderón de la Barca 29 (CB 29), Calderón de la Barca 30 (CB 30), Amsterdam 307, Michelet 50, Cicerón 1 and 2 – has been part of an exercise in which construction has become a way of doing research, of asking broader questions that transcend specific plots of land, regulations or the typology at hand.

His building CB 29 in Colonia Polanco (2007) illustrates this type of larger-scale assemblage, which began with the "Tetris game" structure

Apartment Building Alfonso Reyes 58

of his building on Alfonso Reyes Avenue and was further developed in the low-income housing projects in Oaxaca and single-family dwellings in remote landscapes – like the one in Desierto de los Leones or the project for the "House for Silence". From the most restrictive urban conditions, in terms of regulations and dimensions, to the most utopic and environmentally aware possibilities, Dellekamp's introspective architecture submits forms to

Apartment Building CB30

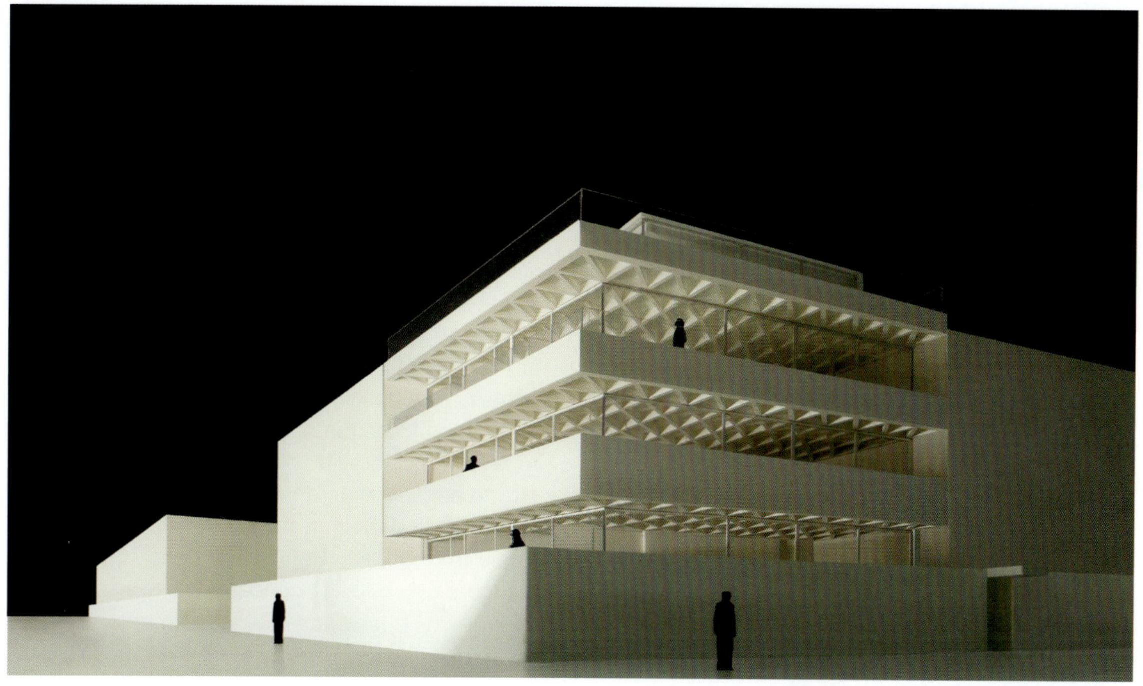

Apartment Building Model, Ciceron II

harsh testing. His architecture is a way of questioning major themes that find their logic on common sense and timelessness. Implicitly involving a revision of the city and its context, his work implies intellectual risk as much as introspection.

The project for CB 29 represents a synthesis of recurring themes in Dellekamp's work: fill-void sequences, insinuated complexity, spaces understood in section views and developed through matrixes or "Tetris game" arrangements. The formal exploration and the freedom allowed by the Alfonso Reyes project (a lot with three open sides and a permit to build up to 21 meters in height) is put to the test in the narrower conditions of CB 29 (a plot tightly bounded on three sides with a maximum construction height of 9 meters). If the first building has "everything," the latter one has only the "essential". In CB 29 the open-closed, fill-void system is simplified, while the importance of an inner courtyard or garden is enhanced. Here the sequence of gardens becomes a main theme and no longer a mere supplement. The interest in craftsmanship and details also becomes fundamental: it is a work full of subtle inflexions – slightly skewed angles to increase perspective views, corners cut to introduce natural light, corridors that widen

Apartment Building Michelet 50

almost unnoticeably, spaces whose every corner has been given careful thought many times over. Subtleties, obsessions that today Dellekamp might even consider idle, add meaning to a work that is simple and light, yet feels well crafted and sculpted.

As with the rest of his work, CB 29 possesses a clear and intelligible structural form. The four-level building stands out clearly against the landscape because of its simple forms, yet, at the same time, it is highly respectful of its context. The building allows the surrounding vegetation to be the protagonist and appears to be of much smaller scale because of the strong horizontality of its glass façade, which, depending on the sun's position and refraction, tends to disappear. Behind apparently simple solutions the building conceals its true complexity. It is impossible to imagine such complexity just by looking at its external façade. Its intricacies only become apparent when one goes through the building itself, especially in the different sections of its three apartment units, developed on two floors each. A particular sense of depth, achieved through the inner courtyard, is not visible from the outside either. This wild empty space separates the public areas of each apartment (facing the front of the lot) from the private areas (at the back), giving each space a double view to the lush gardens. Making the most of the permit to build taller structures at the back of the lot, the apartment on the top floor opens onto a terrace that reminds the user of the urban environment surrounding the complex.

Dellekamp's architecture can be understood as a puzzle that requires precise solutions, powerful schemes capable of organizing the layout and volume as well as the main concept of each project. In CB 29, a rectangle with an empty space in the center created by the courtyard thus becomes a frame surrounding the lot's entire perimeter, leaving the service areas on the courtyards lateral sides. The façades surrounding the empty central garden are made of a combination of transparent and translucent glass, arranged to provide differing degrees of privacy to each level, deterring the views between apartments. The façades' modulation responds in plan to the matrixes used to modulate the spaces, subsequently introducing some type of "accident," like an extra room at an upper level, a sudden double height, or a column placed almost at random. The main façade's rhythm is also interrupted by these incisions, where an angled cut generates a large opening of light or a double height towards the living room. These triangular cuts, clad with the same wood that is used in each apartment stand out when seen from the street. As if they were screens of wood and light, they are the sole gesture altering the order of the façade's glass surface, on the exterior of an architecture that tends to downplay the importance of façades.

The project is structured by regulations (such as height, separation from the neighboring constructions, parking space layout, maximum construction surface…) but then seeks a spatial complexity that seems shaped with ease and precision. CB 29 represents an ongoing story. It could be said that this project is several works in one: one more step in Dellekamp's search to provide an absolute objectivity to his architecture. His idea is to translate each project's program into a clear, quantifiable equation – exalting its abstract condition – concealing the intensity in details and personal commitment in his work. The use of ideal grids capable of absorbing the different demands of the project make it possible to justify, at the same time, the architect's passions and obsessions as well as the rejection of any indulgence.

Dellekamp's increasingly refined architecture aims at sophisticating construction techniques. Shunning the possibility of repeating himself in subsequent projects – for instance with CB 30, which had similar conditions and was built almost simultaneously in the same block– Dellekamp matches the spatial structure with the load-bearing one, so that the construction process leads to the final concept of the finished work. CB 29 is a clear example of the desire to derive and generate the building's geometry from the constructive system; such intention has given order –as well as differentiation– to

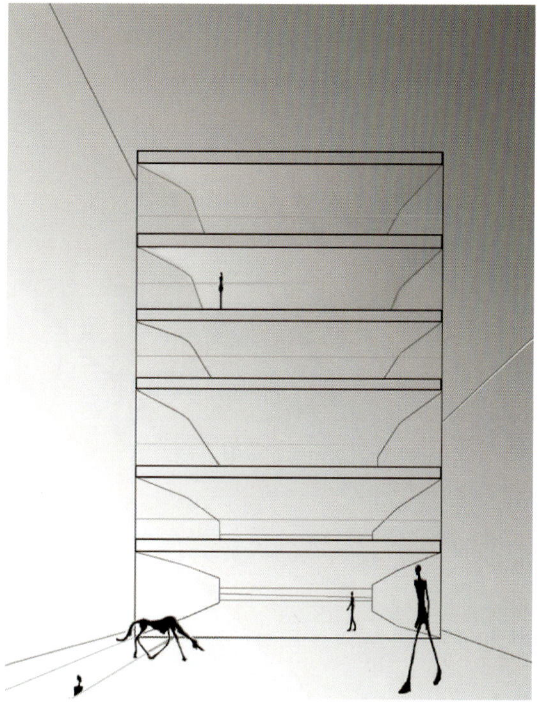

Left: Apartment Building Michelet 50
Right: Apartment Building Amsterdam 307

his projects. With buildings that have implicit constructive systems, he is expanding the arena of formal experimentation, constantly introducing a new challenge or a new game. Far from boasting technical prowess, his interest lies in emphasizing constructive coherence. His rigorously logical buildings are also full of a strong affection for craftsmanship. The projects' components, reduced to a sort of elementary "material innocence," contrast with the sophistication of his work. It is a reserved elegance; as one strolls along the quiet Calle Calderón de la Barca, next to Polanco's park, the two buildings – located at either edge – are almost imperceptible, gradually becoming remarkable for their simplicity.

By sharing the responsibility and ideas for the

Roof Garden CB29

project with its users, Dellekamp enables its users to identify themselves with the building. He has a special sensibility to interpret the relationships established between users, architecture, environment and city, which gives his work a natural feel. Dellekamp has characteristically sieved his influences through an abstract and universal form of thinking, which, in turn, has enabled him to test, overcome, and modify such influences. It is a codified architecture, full of hints and occasional winks to his great "masters." He would probably remark, like Álvaro Siza, "What I appreciate and look for most in architecture is clarity, as much as I do not appreciate simplicity." From him, Dellekamp learned to submit a common piece to certain tensions that would alter, deform and enrich it. On the other hand, he has drawn from contemporary Dutch architects an analytic dimension and abstraction, just as he has borrowed from the architecture of João Vilanova Artigas its authenticity and sensual character. Although he got tired of Luis Barragán's work very early on, he learned from him the use of natural light, the scenographic appeal of spaces, and landscape integration. After Barragán, who is known as the master of color, Dellekamp's work, as well as the rest of Mexican architects from his generation, shies away from the use of color. However, there is a contemplative streak in Barragan's work that Dellekamp has undoubtedly introduced into his own. In an effort to revisit history, Dellekamp makes certain

House of Elza Berquó, Villanova Artigas

traits his own to the point of transforming them into something else. The layout of the CB 29 building bears a certain resemblance to the scheme for Elza Berquó's house at Sao Paulo, designed by Vilanova Artigas in 1967, but in Dellekamp, however, this is a result of a product intimately linked to its volumetric solution and the surrounding context, so much so that the building gives the sensation of being an excavated space instead of a glass box. Once inside, one forgets the sense of being in a large building and feels the intimacy of an individual dwelling, a house open to the landscape, yet profoundly secluded.

The relation of Dellekamp's work to the intense pace of the city is fundamental to understand the manner in which his architecture is sheltered, while simultaneously participating with its urban condition. The importance given to the use of emptiness, silence, and the purity of spaces, therefore, is as relevant as the dynamic character of his architecture. Using clearly differentiated elements to produce a highly polished product, CB 29 provides a broader insight to an architecture that goes beyond common immediacy. Dellekamp's work is defined by that which exists at the middle ground between tension and equilibrium. His work is halfway between austerity and sensualism, between manufacturing and craftsmanship, collectivity and intimacy, past and future, between Mexico and the rest of the world. It is an architectural style that is sober, as much as it is expressive.

cb29

CB29 Apartments
Yaoci Pardo

This three-apartment four-storey building is at the heart of Mexico City's high-end Polanco neighborhood. Polanco's residential hub is notable for its cultural diversity, its upscale hotels, restaurants, designer shops, boutiques, art galleries, parks and tree-shaded walkways, as well as for housing embassies, international organizations, and corporate business.

The design of this residential building rests on three garden areas that give a lush feel to each apartment. Two of these gardens flank the building in the street setback and the private backyard where there is a large oak tree. The third one is a courtyard that provides a fresh indoor view and natural light. This enclosure gives a luxurious sense of promenade within each apartment. The building also has a living roof offering a lookout towards the street.

The gardens gently define three linear sections in the building: public area at the front, service area in the middle, and private area at the back. The hallway facade touring around the courtyard furnishes the living space with the quiet presence of nature thanks to its glass paneling. The combination of transparent glass, in a public living area, and translucent U-glass, in the service and bedroom sections, preserves privacy in the courtyard's semi-public space where needed.

The challenge posed by the client was to give each apartment a unique home-feel. In our design approach, the strict construction policies played a fundamental role since the building could not surpass 9 meters height at street level. Different multi-storey triangular cuts were made to avoid continuous facade floor plans: the apartments were projected beyond a storey in certain areas, and that produced for each residence a unique interior space playing on a rhythm of double-heights. We managed to add a fourth storey in the private section of the building by way of a diagonal arrangement of bedrooms from apartment to apartment. Thus each residential apartment enjoys partial floor use of a second storey in its back section.

The apartment building makes a modern and playful interpretation of the traditional courtyard dwelling, accomplishing a singular home experience for each residence.

3-L

2-L

1-L

Above Left: Organizational and structural diagrams.
Above Right & Opposite: Model.

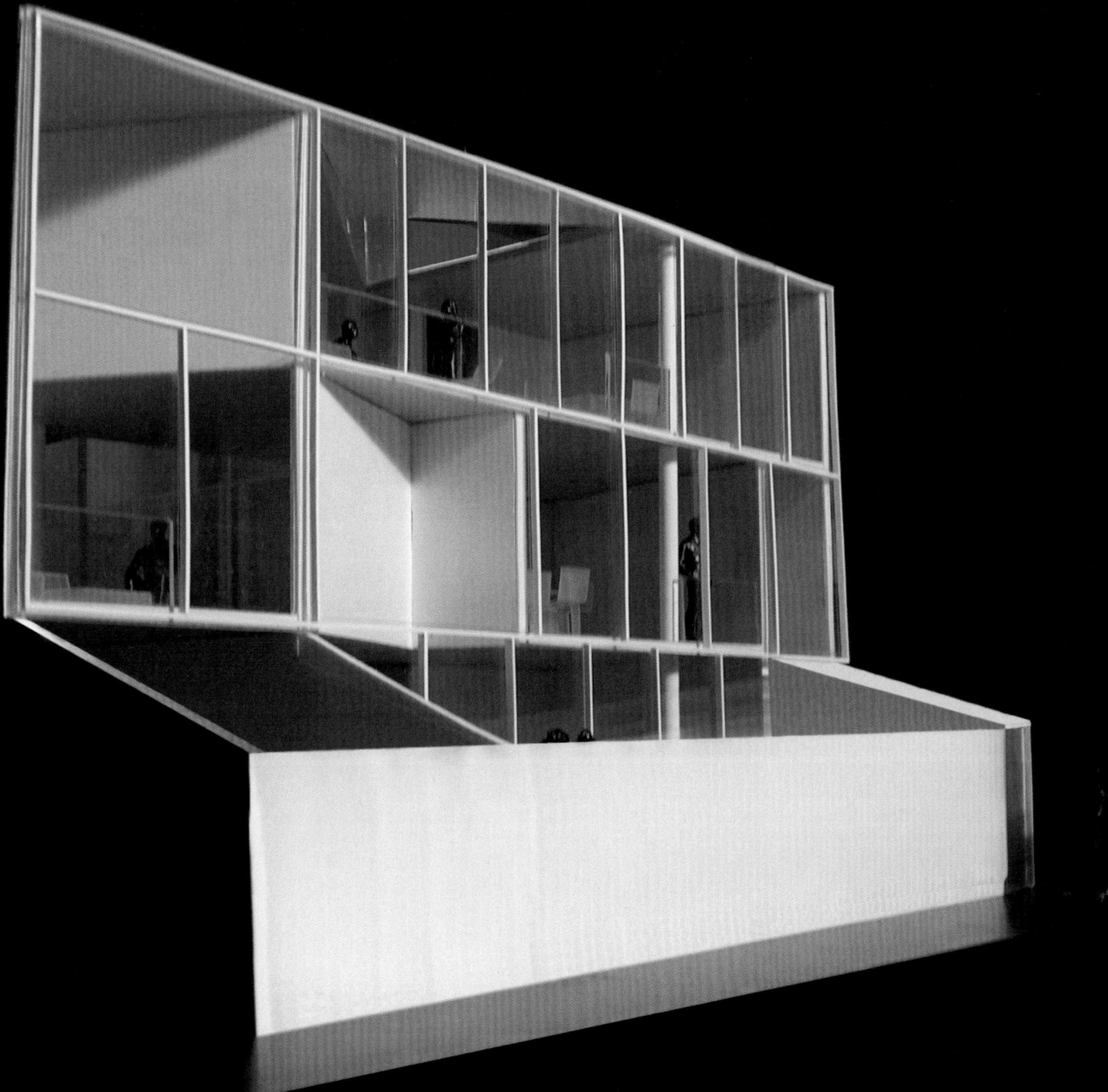

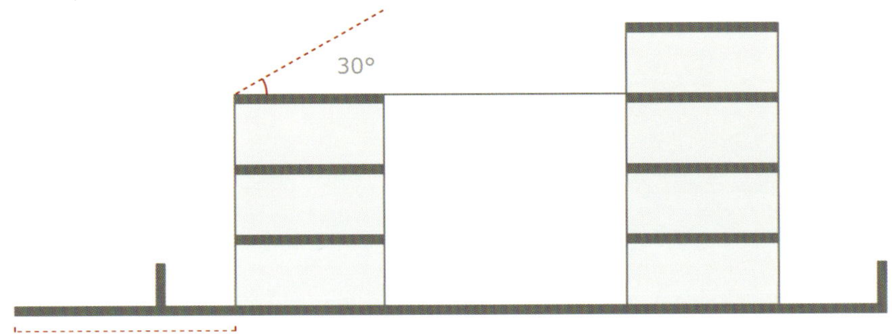

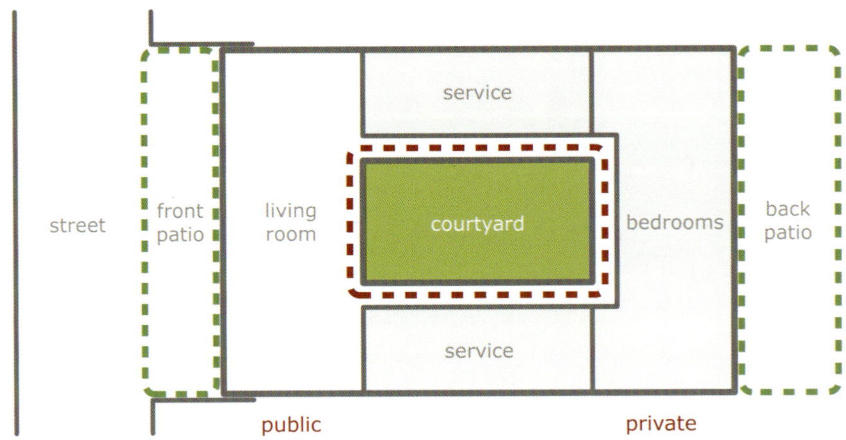

Above and Opposite: Floor Plan CB29

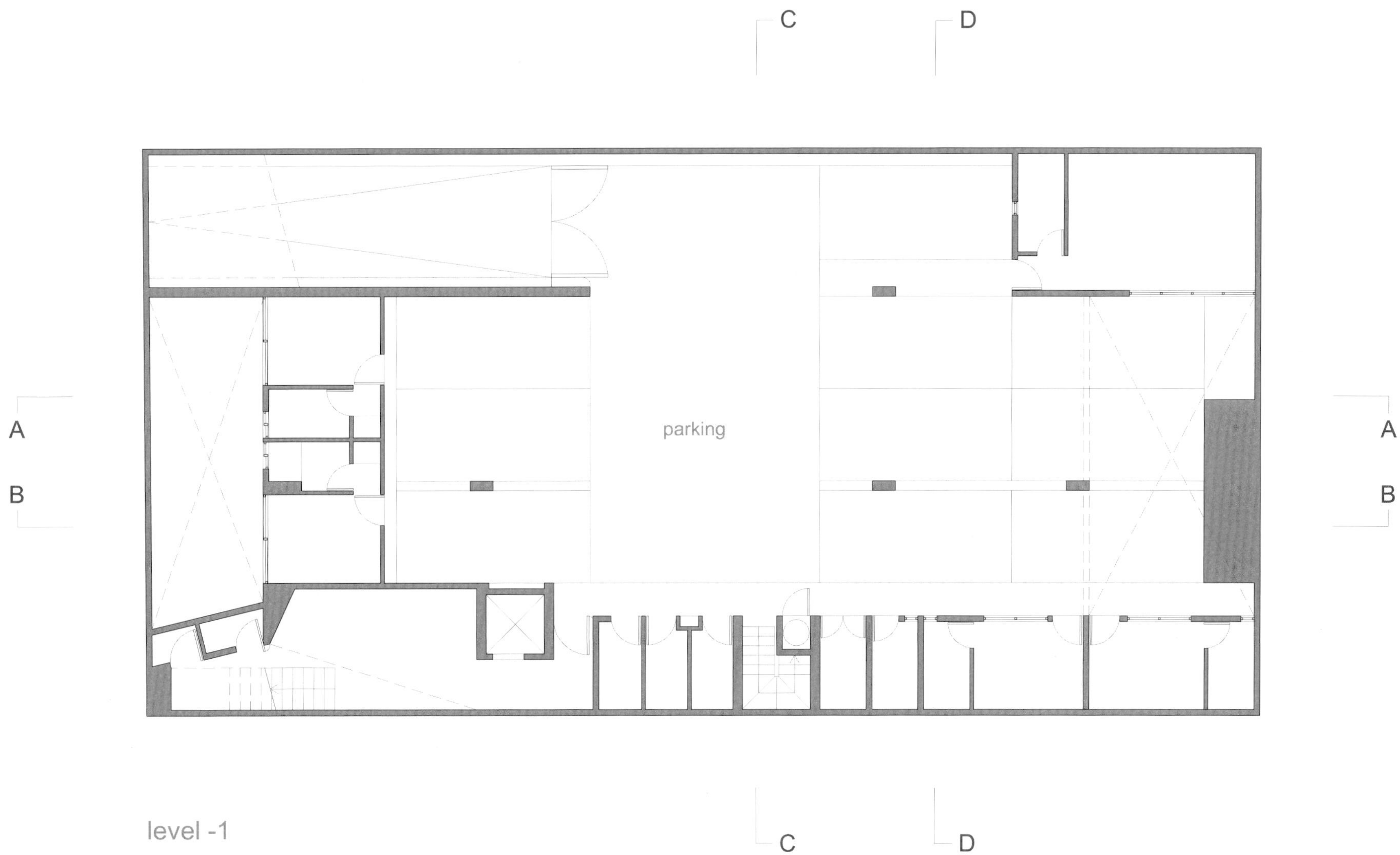

level -1

Above: Floor Plan, Ground.
Opposite: Floor Plan, First.

level 2

Above: Floor Plan, Third.
Opposite: Floor Plan, Fourth.

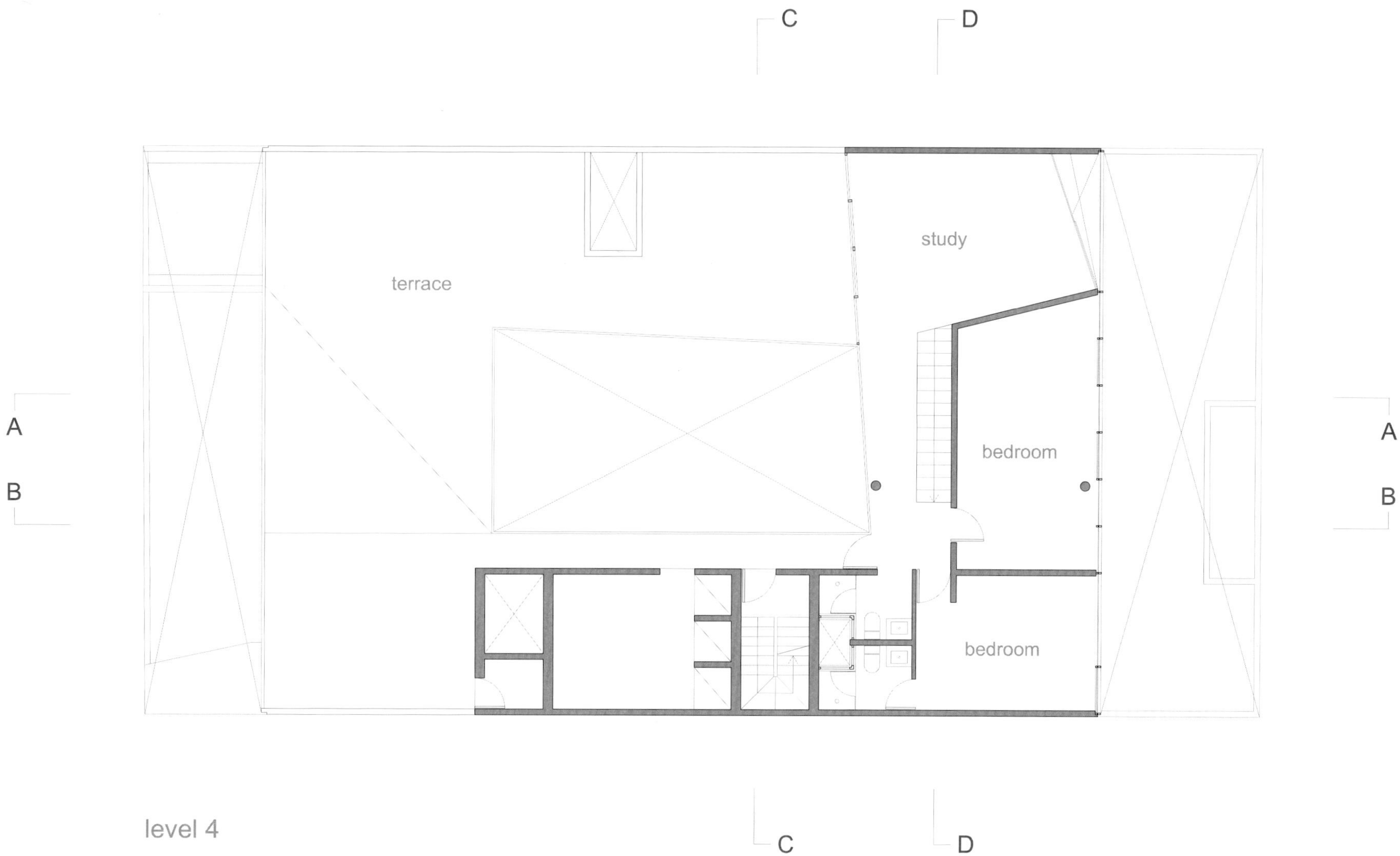

level 4

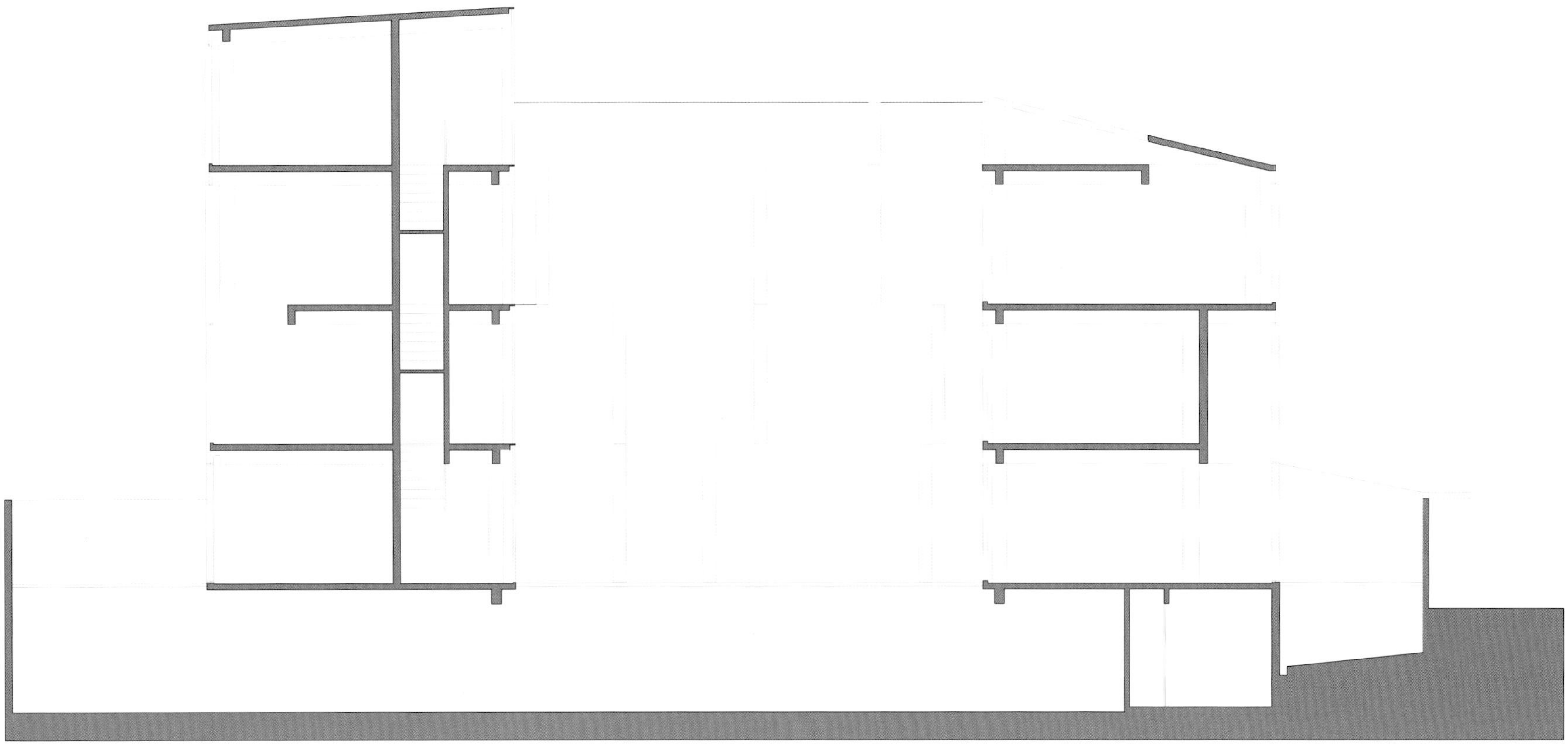

Above: Section A.
Opposite: Section B.

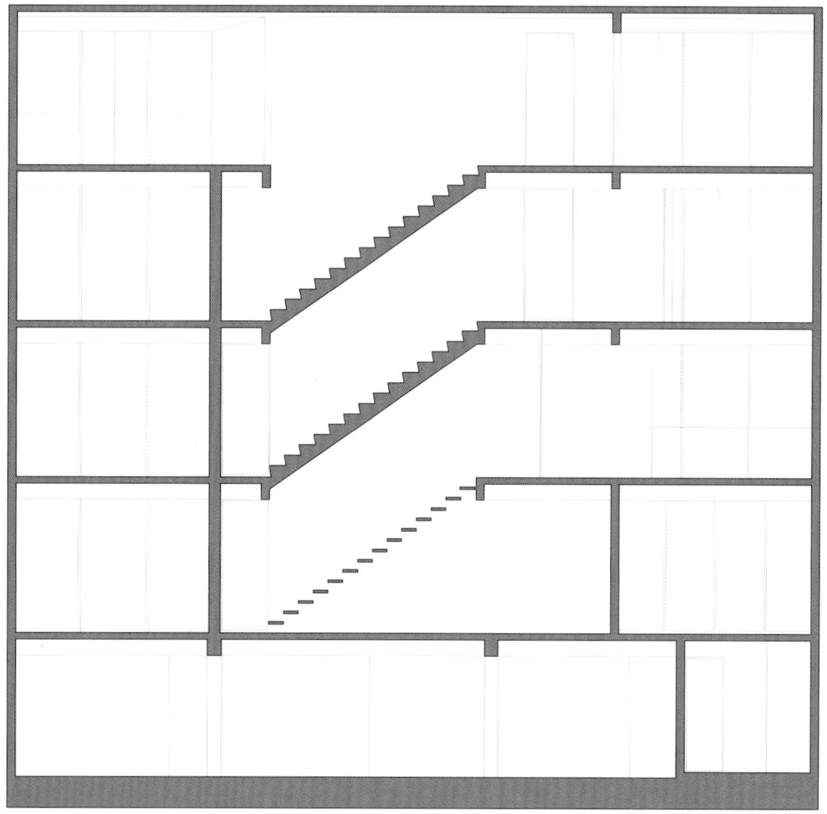

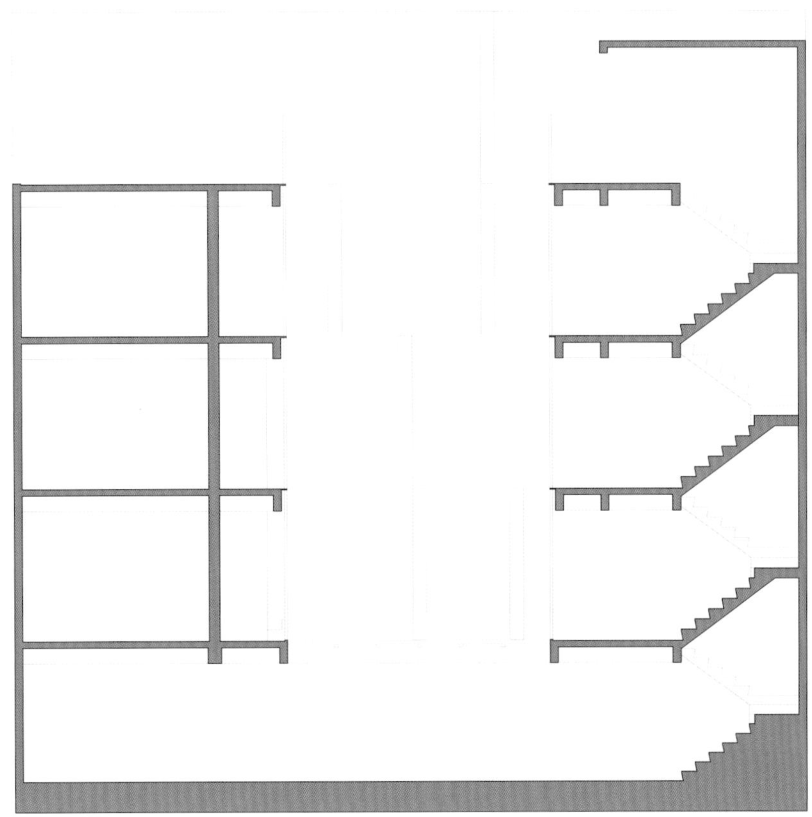

Above: Section B.
Opposite: Section C.

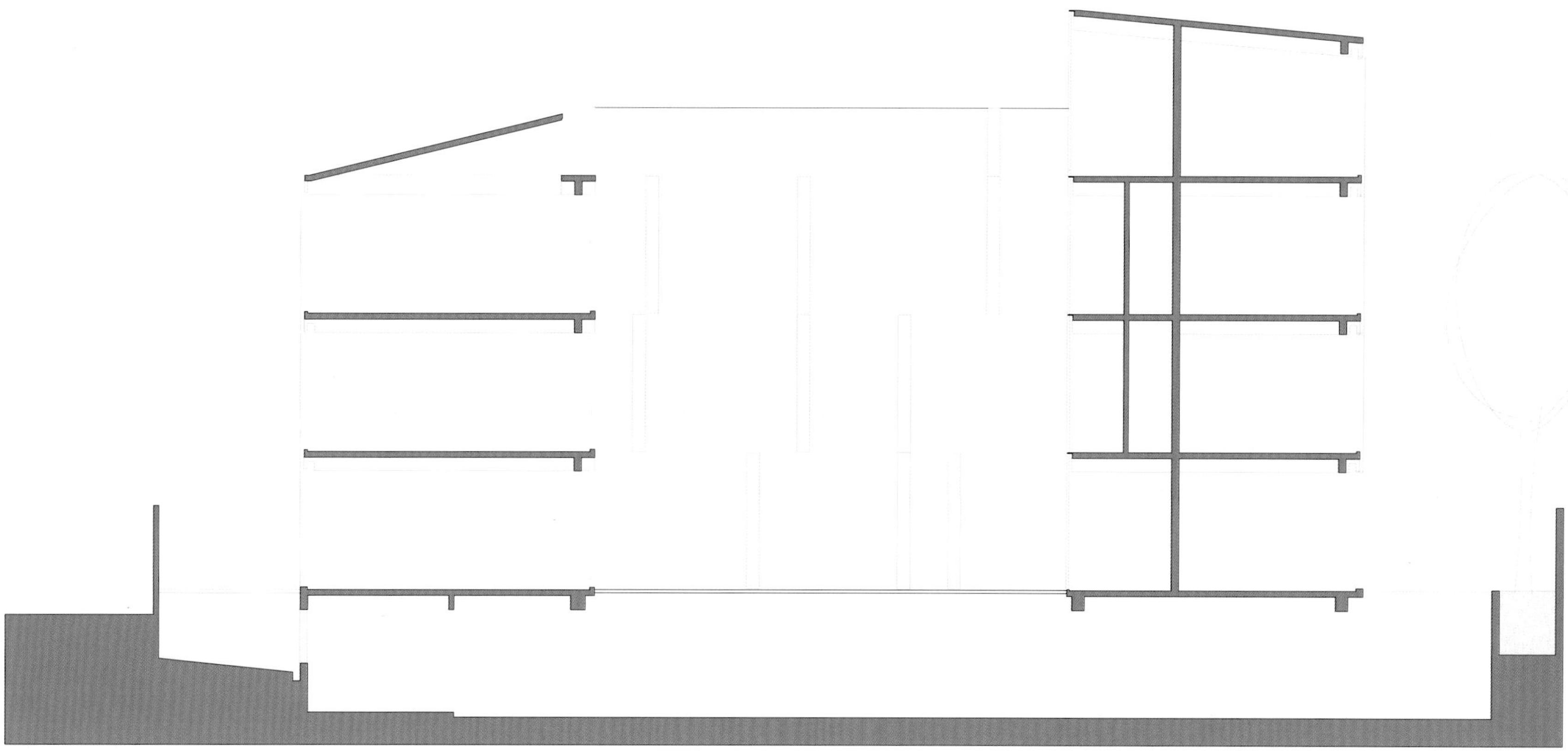

Above: East Elevation.
Opposite: West Elevation.

cb29

Jale

Ahora Polanco ya es VIP
Cinépolis VIP

Biographies

Architects

Tatiana Bilbao
Tatiana Bilbao, born in Mexico City in 1972, studied Architecture and Urbanism in Universidad Iberoamericana. Runs since 2004 a multidisciplinary office that has architectural design as its main practice; the studio analyzes urban and social crisis, as well as rigid codes of communication and telematics to use them as design tools. Through these strands and creating a climate of collaboration where there are various disciplinary resonances in technical areas, theoretical and artistic, the office, regenerates spaces "humanized" to be aware and react to global capitalism, opening up niches for cultural and economic development.

Having done projects mainly in Mexico, the office has done buildings, exhibitions and interventions all over the world, manly China, Spain, France and the USA.

Tatiana Bilbao has been invited professor and lecturing in places such as ETH Zurich, AA in London, University of Cambridge, UT in Austin, Dessau among others.

Prizes include Emerging Voices 2009 of the Architectural League of New York and exhibitions include Centre Georges Pompidou, Paris, France, ICM in San Antonio, Texas, Venice Biennale.

Derek Dellekamp
Derek Dellekamp studied architecture at the Universidad Iberoamericana in Mexico City, where he obtained his BArch in 1997. He established his office Dellekamp Arquitectos in 1999.

His work has been widely published and exhibited in Mexico, Greece, Austria, and in the ART Basel, and also as in the Biennale of Venice in 2008. The apartment buildings CB 29 and CB 30 were awarded the International Prize of Architecture in 2008, and in 2010 his social housing project Tlacolula received the Silver Medal at the XI Mexican Biennale of Architecture.

The Ruta del Peregrino (Guadalajara), jointly curated and directed with the office of Tatiana Bilbao, received the first prize in the CEMEX Building Award 2010 and in the same year the Centre Pompidou selected the project to be part of their collection of architecture. In 2010, he was honored by the Mexican Association of Architects with the CAM-SAM Bicentenario al Mérito Profesional.

The practice of Dellekamp Arquitectos is also involved in ongoing architectural research of social housing in Mexico, currently funded by the FONCA foundation scholarship.

Authors

Fernanda Canales (México, 1974)
Graduated with honors in 1997 in architecture from the Universidad Iberoamericana she earned her MA from the Universidad Politécnica de Cataluña (Barcelona, 2001). She is currently completing a PHD in the Escuela Técnica Superior de Arquitectura de Madrid. She is the recipient of the "Young Creators" fellowship from the Fondo Nacional para la Cultura y las Artes (FONCA) and has received awards such as Premio Cemex and Colegio de Arquitectos Bienal.

Since 1997 she has her own independent architecture and research practice based in México City, focusing in housing, educational and cultural programs. Her firm has won several competitions, including the new CEDIM Campus in Monterrey as well as the competition for a theater complex in Guadalajara.

Her books include *Arquitectos del Siglo XX en México*, *Central de Arquitectura*, and *Espacios Culturales de Abraham Zabludovsky*. Recent exhibits include: Museo de Arte Moderno Mexico City, Rotterdam Biennale, Bienal de Arquitectura de Sao Paulo and the Venice Biennale. She has taught at the Universidad Iberoamericana in the Design and Urbanism program, at the CMAS Master´s program as well as in the UNAM.

Patrick Charpenel
Born in 1967 in Guadalajara, he lives and works there.

With a degree in philosophy he has carried out an intense task as curator, highlighting the paradoxes and ambiguities of the contemporary world.

In 2009 he curated the exhibition Franz West Elefante Blanco at the Museo Tamayo Arte Contemporáneo, Mexico City. He curated the retrospective Gabriel Orozco at the Museo del Palacio de Bellas Artes, Mexico, in 2006. He was a guest curator for the 2009 Art Projects section at the Art Basel Miami Beach Fair, and invited to curate the 2010 Summer International Artist-in-Residence 10.2, Artpace, San Antonio, Texas.

Since 2005 he has been the curator and coordinator of the Botanical Garden art project in Culiacan, Mexico. He writes critical texts in specialized magazines.

Yaocí Pardo
Yaocí Pardo is an author, editor, and translator, and writes for cultural magazines. She is a Ph.D. candidate in Comparative Literature at The University of Western Ontario. Her areas of specialization include Western Philosophy and Post-Structuralist Theory in the Visual Arts and Literature. She has conducted research on memory and various types of discontinuous prose (aphorisms, maxims, proverbs, slogans, fragments); as well as on medical and legal practices in the Elizabethan stage, discursive practices of new writing technologies, and allegorical uses of architectural space. Currently, Pardo teaches Critical Theory and English Literature at the Universidad Iberoamericana in Mexico City.

Wilfried Wang
Wilfried Wang is the O'Neil Ford Centennial Professor in Architecture at The University of Texas at Austin. Together with Barbara Hoidn, he is founder of the office of Hoidn Wang Partner, Berlin.

Wang studied architecture in London, where he was in partnership with John Southall. In 1979 he was founding co-editor of 9H magazine and co-director of the 9H Gallery from 1985 to 1990. From 1995 to 2000 he was the director of the German Architecture Museum.

He taught at the Polytechnic of North London, University College London, ETH Zurich, Harvard University and the University of Navarra.

Wang is the author and editor of various architectural publications. He has served on competition and award juries, is the chairman of the Schelling Architecture Foundation and a member of the design review board of Munich Airport. He is an honorary member of the Federation of German Architects and a foreign member of the Royal Swedish Academy of Arts. He holds an honorary doctorate from the Royal Institute of Technology, Stockholm and is a member of the Academy of the Arts Berlin.

Project Credits and Information

Ajijic House

Architect	Tatiana Bilbao
Project Leader	Thorsten Englert
Team	Damian Figueras, Marco Robles, Adriana De Carvalho, Edgar Sanchez
Client	Viviane Charpenel
Structural Engineers	Ing. Jorge A. Cardena C. Moncad S.A. de C.V.
Construction Company	Cabrera & Asociados
Construction Supervision	Tatiana Bilbao S.A.
Specialist Suppliers	Cynthia Gutierrez Alvarez Marco Rountree Rodlofo Diaz
Site Area	2390 m^2
Total Constructed	316 m^2
Ground Floor	273 m^2
First Floor	43 m^2
Project Period	October 2009 - May 2010
Construction Period	May 2010 - March 2011

CB29 Apartments

Architect	Derek Dellekamp
Project Leader:	Aisha Ballesteros
Team:	Rodrigo Alcocer, Alejandro Santillanes, Tania Velazco, Alin Vázquez, Victor Jaime
Client	Familia González Ulloa
Structural Engineers	Ing. Juan Paulino Zaenz + assistant, Ing. Ramon Cueto Castillo (INTRA)
Construction Company	INTRA Construcciones S.A. de C.V.
Construction Supervision	Dellekamp Arquitectos
Specialist Suppliers	Ambiente Arquitectos
Site Area	435 m^2
Total Constructed Floor Area	1405 m^2
Project Period	January - April 2006
Construction period	April 2006 – January 2008

Selected Bibliography

CB29 Apartments

2008 The International Architecture Awards: The Chicago Athenaeum: APARTMENT BUILDING 2008

ARCH MANUAL, AADCU Program, , edit. Bruce Q. Lan, Beijing 2010, p.96-99

EGG 09, SINGLE HOUSES, September 2007, Taiwan, p. 90-91.

ION+, Canada, August 2008- n° 50, p. 2-3.

Summa+, VIVIENDA COLECTIVA, Argentina, N° 94, p.34-39

Casabella, Italy, n° 738 p.58-63.

C3topic House II, Korea, p.139|p.143.

Photo Credits

Cover Photographs: Iwan Baan

Dante Busquets: pages 77, 80, 104, 106, 112, 113, 116, 117, 122, 125, 127

Iwan Baan: pages 1, 4, 10, 11, 12, 18, 50, 51, 52, 53, 54, 55, 56, 57, 58, 59, 60, 61, 62, 63, 64, 65, 66, 67, 68, 69, 70, 71, 72, 73 82, 100, 102, 103, 110, 111, 118, 119, 120, 121, 123, 124, 126, 128, 129, 130, 131, 132, 133, 134, 135, 136, 137, 139

Oscar Necoechea: pages 76, 102, 107, 109, 114, 115

Sandra Pereznieto: pages 78, 79